Cultural Criticism

A Primer of Key Concepts

Arthur Asa Berger

Foundations of Popular Culture Vol. *4*

SAGE Publications
International Educational and Professional Publisher
Thousand Oaks   London   New Delhi

For information address:

 SAGE Publications, Inc.
2455 Teller Road
Thousand Oaks, California 91320

SAGE Publications Ltd.
6 Bonhill Street
London EC2A 4PU
United Kingdom

SAGE Publications India Pvt. Ltd.
M-32 Market
Greater Kailash I
New Delhi 110 048 India

Printed in the United States of America

Library of Congress Cataloging-in-Publication Data

Berger, Arthur Asa, 1933-
    Cultural criticism : a primer of key concepts / Arthur Asa Berger
        p. cm. — (Foundations of popular culture ; vol. 4)
    Includes bibliographical references (p.   ) and index.
    ISBN 0-8039-5733-5 (cl). — ISBN 0-8039-5734-3 (pb)
    1. Culture. 2. Criticism. 3. Communism and culture.
4. Semiotics—Social aspects. 5. Psychoanalysis and culture.
6. Sociology—Methodology. I. Title. II. Series.
CB151.B386   1995
306.4—dc20   94-35085

95 96 97 98 99   10 9 8 7 6 5 4 3 2

Sage Production Editor: Astrid Virding

Cultural Criticism

FOUNDATIONS OF POPULAR CULTURE

Series Editor: GARTH S. JOWETT
University of Houston

The study of popular culture has now become a widely accepted part of the modern academic curriculum. This increasing interest has spawned a great deal of important research in recent years, and the field of "cultural studies" in its many forms is now one of the most dynamic and exciting in modern academia. Each volume in the **Foundations of Popular Culture Series** will introduce a specific issue fundamental to the study of popular culture, and the authors have been given the charge to write with clarity and precision and to examine the subject systematically. The editorial objective is to provide an important series of "building block" volumes that can stand by themselves or be used in combination to provide a thorough and accessible grounding in the field of cultural studies.

1. **The Production of Culture: Media and the Urban Arts**
   by **Diana Crane**

2. **Popular Culture Genres: Theories and Texts**
   by **Arthur Asa Berger**

3. **Rock Formation: Music, Technology, and Mass Communication**
   by **Steve Jones**

4. **Cultural Criticism: A Primer of Key Concepts**
   by **Arthur Asa Berger**

Contents

Series Editor's Introduction

One of the most interesting and also challenging aspects of the emergence of popular culture studies in the last two decades has been the creation of a specific argot by scholars to describe the complex nature of cultural activities. This argot, replete with neologisms and often arcane language, has been both praised for its ability to creatively conceptualize new synergies of cultural interaction and also condemned for its impenetrability and obfuscation.

The neophyte student of popular culture who is asked to read many popular cultural texts is often faced with having to work with a dictionary in one hand and his or her text in the other. In many cases the dictionary itself is not enough to provide a definition of how the usage of words and phrases have been shifted to meet the needs of popular culture scholars. For example, what is the difference between a "problem" and a "problematic"? No current dictionary makes this cultural criticism usage clear to the inexperienced reader. What does "hegemony" mean? How is the concept of "ideology" applied? Perhaps most difficult of all, what is "postmodernism," and why should anyone care about it?

This book by Arthur Berger, who has been one of the most prolific of all writers in the field of popular culture, examines these words and concepts from a perspective of more than three decades of experience. Throughout, Dr. Berger's wit and ability to "cut through" helps the reader to understand the new argot, while at the same time providing concrete examples of its application. There are bound to be a few readers who will take exception to some of his definitions and explanations, but this is the contentious nature of the field of popular culture studies at this point in time. However, this book is an extremely valuable addition to the field, in that it offers an introduction to complex ideas in a way that is itself very accessible.

There will be other attempts to "define the territory" of popular culture in the future, but Arthur Asa Berger's book will stand as an important achievement for others to emulate. The volume can be a valuable addition to a variety of courses on popular culture, or it can be used as a primary text for introductory courses on popular culture. Whatever its intended use, students will be both charmed and informed by Dr. Berger's perspectives.

—GARTH JOWETT
Series Editor

Acknowledgments

I would like to thank Sophy Craze, my editor at Sage Publications, for her encouragement, and Garth Jowett, the editor of the **Foundations of Popular Culture** series, for his support and friendship over the years. Mitch Allen, Sage's northern California editor, has been a good friend and has helped me come up with ideas for books for Sage for quite a while. He has also rejected an inhumane number of my manuscripts. As he once put it, "I've rejected better men than you, Arthur." Rather than writing new books for Mitch to reject, I have now taken to sending him manuscripts he previously rejected, with new titles, for him to reject again—or maybe accept, in a moment of weakness or madness? One always hopes!

This is, it turns out, my sixth book with Sage Publications. They probably deserve some kind of a medal! Or maybe I do? (Maybe we all do?) Whatever the case, I have had wonderful experiences with the people there—with the editorial staff, the production staff, and the marketing staff—so, even as I sit writing this, in the back of my mind I'm thinking up ideas for new books.

My colleagues in the Broadcast and Electronic Communication Arts Department at San Francisco State University have provided a congenial, supportive, and exciting place to work, and my students have endured my courses in criticism (where I discuss *The Prisoner*, blondness, professional wrestling, and teeth and hairstyles as signs, and explain how the Washington monument is a phallic symbol) with stoicism, skepticism, and a good-natured kind of puzzlement and bemusement.

LITERARY THEORY

SOCIOLOGY

SOCIOLOGY

Tre

psychoanalytic Theory

MARXISM

Berger 94

1

An Introduction to Cultural Criticism

Writing a little book about a big subject is an extremely difficult thing to do. It is much harder than writing a big book about a little subject, which seems to be the standard operating procedure for many writers nowadays. Somehow, over the past 30 years, I have taken on the task—or perhaps it would be a bit more accurate to say that I have ended up with the task—of explaining complicated subjects in clear and relatively simple (but not simplistic, I hope) terms, and have done so in a number of little books on big subjects. It takes a good deal of effort, I might add, to write books on complicated subjects that are accessible and that readers find interesting.

The *Mission Impossible* Dream

I have this recurring dream. It is 3:00 A.M. and I find myself, somehow, in a deserted building on a college campus. I walk into a large, empty lecture hall, where I see a tape recorder on a table. Beside it is a manila envelope. I walk over to the table and press the button that turns on the tape recorder. This is what I hear:

> Your mission, if you accept it, Arthur, is to explain cultural criticism and cultural studies in easy-to-understand terms. You will write an

accessible book that deals with many of the important concepts and ideas in literary theory, semiotics, psychoanalytic thought, Marxist thought, and sociological thought for readers who may have little or no background in these areas. We have assembled an international team of experts to help you carry out your mission. Their photographs are found in the sealed envelope you see before you. If you are taken prisoner by the postmodernists, neither your dean, your department chair, nor your editor will accept responsibility for you or aid in obtaining your release. This tape will self-destruct in three seconds.

Three seconds later, the tape goes POOF and burns up. I pick up the envelope and tear it open. In it are photographs of a number of people: Karl Marx, Sigmund Freud, Ferdinand de Saussure, Mikhail Bakhtin, Michel Foucault, Jacques Derrida, and a dozen others. "Good," I think. "I've got an international team of superstar philosophers, psychologists, and cultural theorists to help me!"

Then I wake, in a cold sweat. "Good Lord, what have I gotten myself into?" I ask myself. I then have a breakfast of orange juice, oatmeal with hot milk, yogurt, a caffé latte, and toast. I skim the *San Francisco Chronicle* and *New York Times*. Then, with a sigh, I get up from the breakfast table and walk slowly to a room lined with books, where a computer sits on a desk. I turn on the computer and start typing.

Cultural Criticism and Cultural Studies

Cultural criticism is an activity, not a discipline per se, as I interpret things. That is, cultural critics apply the concepts and theories addressed in this book, in varying combinations and permutations, to the elite arts, popular culture, everyday life, and a host of related topics. Cultural criticism is, I suggest, a multidisciplinary, interdisciplinary, pandisciplinary, or metadisciplinary undertaking, and cultural critics come from, and use ideas from, a variety of disciplines. Cultural criticism can involve literary and aesthetic theory and criticism, philosophical thought, media analysis, popular cultural criticism, interpretive theories and disciplines (semiotics, psychoanalytic theory, Marxist theory, sociological and anthropological theory, and so on), communication studies, mass media research, and various other means of making sense of contemporary (and not so contemporary) culture and society.

The term *cultural studies* is not new; in 1971, the Centre for Contemporary Cultural Studies at the University of Birmingham started publishing a journal, *Working Papers in Cultural Studies*, which dealt with media, popular culture, subcultures, ideological matters, literature, semiotics, gender-related issues, social movements, everyday life, and a variety of other topics. I regarded the establishment of the journal as very exciting, for it showed that the people at the University of Birmingham were taking popular culture and the media seriously. Unfortunately, the journal did not last very long. It did, however, have a considerable impact, and it provided a kind of umbrella term that covers what scholars from many disciplines now do—what I have described as *cultural criticism*.

One of the major problems with cultural criticism is that the vocabulary used in criticism, analysis, and interpretation has become incredibly recondite and highly technical. In many cases it is absolutely opaque. When cultural critics communicate with one another in scholarly books and articles, they do so, generally speaking, in a language that tends to be obscure, full of what the layperson would describe as jargon. It is often extremely difficult to understand.

On Technical Language

Shortly before I started writing this book, I had a conversation with a friend about cultural criticism. "Who reads this stuff?" he asked. "It's just about unintelligible. I would imagine there's a relatively small number of people who write these crit-speak books and the only people who might want to read them or can understand them are their friends." It was that comment that led me to write this book. Despite the jargon and technical language found in much cultural criticism, many of the writers and theorists in the field have useful and suggestive ideas and concepts to share that people interested in the media, popular culture, and related concerns should find valuable—if, that is, these writers and their theories and concepts can be understood. I felt that I could help make their ideas more intelligible for some readers. Some French writers, such as Jacques Derrida, communicate in a notoriously obscure fashion, and it has even been suggested that Derrida and others write impenetrable and opaque prose on purpose, so that if their ideas are attacked they can always argue that they have actually been misunderstood.

We must realize that many of the authors discussed in this volume are addressing very complicated matters, issues, ideas, and theories, so there is good reason for a certain amount of complexity in their writing. They come from many different countries, from a variety of disciplines, and are also writing, generally speaking, for people with a considerable amount of education who are interested in their ideas. Often the readers of the important theorists also have considerable background in the subject under discussion. The problem, as I have noted, is that these writers are not accessible to large numbers of people who, I believe, would find their ideas interesting and suggestive and would benefit from knowing about them.

Making Complex Ideas Accessible

In this book I present some of the more important concepts used in cultural criticism and explain them as simply and clearly as I can. In doing so, I hope to offer readers the conceptual background they need to understand and do cultural criticism. This book, remember, is a primer; it is meant to provide readers with an overview of cultural criticism, a sense of what cultural critics do and how they do it. I make it a point to present quotations that show how significant terms are used by various influential thinkers—to expose readers to the styles of a number of major writers and

On Concepts

We should not be put off by unfamiliar concepts, but should learn what they mean and how to use them, for it is through concepts (which, when linked together, form disciplines and subject matters) that we make sense of the world. The term *concept* comes from the Latin *concipere*, which means "to conceive." In the current context, a concept is an idea, theory, hypothesis, or notion that someone who is interested in cultural criticism uses to interpret, understand, make sense of, find meaning in, and see relationships in

1. what characters say and do in texts (and what people in real life say and do in their everyday lives);
2. data about the world and the role of institutions in the world;
3. the behavior of individuals and groups of people;
4. the way the human mind, psyche, and body function, and the relationship between the psyche and the body; and
5. the role of texts (works of elite and public art) in the development of individuals and the impact of these texts on society and culture.

thinkers. It is my intention for this book to be readable and accessible for most readers; however, even though this is a primer, I must confess that in some places the going does get rather difficult.

It may be interesting for readers to know where many of the more important thinkers in cultural criticism have come from, so I have constructed Table 1.1—an exercise in what might be called cultural criticism geography. We see that France, Russia, and Germany have produced the lion's share of cultural critics and theorists, though the table is, admittedly, highly selective—it leaves out many important thinkers. It should be noted that many of the thinkers listed in Table 1.1 are not contemporary either.

TABLE 1.1 The Geography of Cultural Criticism: Countries of Origin
of Influential Cultural Studies Theorists (A Selective List)

France	Russia	Germany
Roland Barthes	M. M. Bakhtin	Karl Marx
Claude Lévi-Strauss	L. S. Vygotsky	Max Weber
Michel Foucault	Vladimir Propp	Jürgen Habermas
Louis Althusser	S. Eisenstein	Theodor Adorno
Jacques Lacan	Yuri Lotman	Walter Benjamin
Émile Durkheim	Viktor Shklovsky	Max Horkheimer
Jacques Derrida		Herbert Marcuse
Pierre Bourdieu		Hans-Georg Gadamer
Andre Bazin		Bertolt Brecht
A. J. Greimas		

United States	Canada	England
C. S. Peirce	Marshall McLuhan	Raymond Williams
Noam Chomsky	H. Innis	Stuart Hall
Wilbur Schramm	Northrop Frye	Ludwig Wittgenstein
Roman Jakobson		Richard Hoggart
Victor Turner		Mary Douglas
Clifford Geertz		William Empson
Fredric Jameson		

Switzerland	Austria	Italy
Ferdinand de Saussure	Sigmund Freud	Antonio Gramsci
Carl Jung	Herta Herzog	Umberto Eco

Thinkers Evolve and
Change Their Ideas Over Time

Dealing with the ideas of important theorists is also complicated because we find that theorists often change their ideas over
the years (so we are faced with the issue of which of their works
should be considered most important). We also find that followers of particular theorists often disagree on how to interpret
certain terms, concepts, and theories connected with those theorists. Freud, for example, wrote many books and countless articles and letters that show that he changed his mind about various
concepts as his thinking developed. In the same light, there are

still arguments about what Marx "really" believed. Was he a humanist and moralist, or did he believe in the need for violent revolution? W. H. Auden once said that the words of the dead are "modified in the guts of the living"—to this we can add that the words of the living are also modified in the guts of the living.

There is, of necessity, a certain amount of reductionism or simplification in this book. It is impossible to deal with difficult and extremely complicated concepts such as deconstruction and postmodernism in just a few pages without leaving a great deal out. It is possible, however, to capture the gist of such theories and give readers a pretty good idea of what they are about. I believe that by using quotations judiciously and explaining concepts in language that is relatively easy to understand, I can enable readers to make sense of cultural criticism.

A Useful Analogy

Let me offer an analogy that might be useful here. Assume that you have never been to Europe and are planning a trip there for a few months and hope to visit five or six countries. You might begin to plan your trip by reading a general travel book on Europe. Once you have read it, you can then turn to books on individual countries (such as France), particular areas in individual countries (such as central France), individual cities (such as Paris), and even particular areas of particular cities (such as Montparnasse) to get more detailed information. But you need to get a good overview and some ideas about the best places to go before you start finding out, in depth, about specific countries, areas, and cities.

Readers who want more information about specific concepts, ideas, issues, topics, theories, or theorists connected with cultural criticism should consult the list of suggested further reading that follows the text. Many of the works found there contain their own substantial bibliographies, which will lead interested readers to even more resources. For example, the literature on postmodernism is enormous. A number of the books on this subject reference articles and other books that will provide anyone

A Cultural Critic Always Has a Point of View

Cultural critics don't just criticize out of the blue. They always have some connection to some group or discipline: feminists, Marxists, Freudians, Jungians, conservatives, gays and lesbians, radicals, anarchists, semioticians, sociologists, anthropologists, or some combination of the above. Cultural criticism, then, is always grounded in some perspective on things that the critic (or analyst, if one wishes to avoid the negative connotations of the word *critic*) believes best explains things.

When looking at the academic or disciplinary identities of individuals doing cultural criticism, in many cases there are no problems. They come from literature departments, sociology departments, philosophy departments, and so on. But in the case of communication schools and departments there is a big problem. One is reminded of the story in Swift's *Gulliver's Travels* about the war between Lilliput and Blefescu, which was fought over the correct end from which a person should eat a soft-boiled egg. There is an ongoing dispute about what we should call departments, schools, and colleges devoted to the study of communication. Are they to be called departments, schools, or colleges of *communication* (without an *s*) or departments, schools, or colleges of *communications* (with an *s*)? Or departments, schools, or colleges *for* communication, which is what the Annenberg Schools (at the University of Southern California and the University of Pennsylvania) now call themselves (implying, perhaps, that other schools are against communication)? The Annenberg Schools may be correct, but a number of people find it ironic that these schools identify themselves as *for* communication when their behavior, often, seems to be to the contrary.

The whole thing is a puzzlement.

interested in this aspect of cultural criticism with a huge reading list, and books on various aspects of postmodernism continue to roll off the presses in increasing numbers. One of the best books on postmodernism, Steven Best and Douglas Kellner's *Postmodern Theory* (1991), has a bibliography that lists hundreds of primary and secondary sources.

There is, I should point out, a bit of overlap between this book and my earlier text titled *Media Analysis Techniques* (1991). In that book, however, I do not address literary theory, and I do not explain as many concepts—or go into as much detail about them—as I do in this volume. Also, half of *Media Analysis Techniques* is taken up with applications of the theories presented. This book is different in that it is devoted entirely to concepts and theoretical concerns.

It is my hope that this guidebook will intrigue you, whet your appetite for more in-depth investigation of various concepts and theories, and stimulate your interest in cultural criticism in general. In preparing this book, I have had several goals in mind, among them, that you will gain (a) an appreciation of what cultural criticism has to offer, (b) an understanding of a number of the most basic concepts used in cultural criticism, (c) the tools for investigating in more depth the concepts that interest you, and (d) the ability to become a cultural critic yourself, to use the concepts you have learned to analyze aspects of culture and society that interest you. I urge you to try your hand at this important and fascinating undertaking.

If you start seeing the world around you differently, if you find yourself able to apply what you have learned in this book to the media, to politics, to the arts, to popular culture, and to various aspects of everyday life, this book will have served its purpose.

Aristotle

2

Literary Theory and Cultural Criticism

In this chapter I deal with literary theory, which is one of the most important disciplines or areas of interest relative to cultural studies. My focus is on some of the more important concepts used by literary theorists—concepts that can be applied most immediately to literature but also to culture in general.

Literary theory is very important because it provides a basis for analyzing works. Though some literary theorists go to extremes (or sometimes have their ideas pushed to extremes), privileging the reader over the text and arguing that works of literature (and subliterature) do not exist until they are called into existence by readers and audiences, or suggesting that works are little more than collections of artistic "devices," there is a great deal of controversy and vitality in the field, and this is a very positive sign.

Mimesis and Other Theories of Literature

Mimesis is Latin for "imitation," which is one of the most important theories of art. In his *Poetics,* Aristotle suggests that the arts are based on imitation: "Epic poetry and Tragedy, Comedy also and Dithyrambic poetry, and the music of the flute and of the lyre in most of their forms are all in their general conception modes of imitation" (quoted in Smith & Parks, 1951, p. 28).

If art is an imitation of life, this gives it, M. H. Abrams suggests, a lower status than life itself. In his influential book *The Mirror and the Lamp: Romantic Theory and the Critical Tradition* (1958), Abrams offers four fundamental critical orientations, including mimesis:

1. *Mimetic theories of art:* In Abrams's typology, mimetic art is art that mirrors, or reflects, reality.

2. *Objective theories of art:* According to objective theories of art, rather than imitating reality, art projects its own more or less self-contained reality. It is thus opposed to the mirror and is represented by the lamp: "The 'objective orientation,' which on principle regards the work of art in isolation from all . . . external points of reference, analyzes it as a self-sufficient entity constituted by its parts in their internal relations, and sets out to judge it solely by criteria intrinsic to its own mode of being" (Abrams, 1958, p. 26). This is close to the notion that art exists only for art's sake.

3. *Pragmatic theories of art:* These theories suggest that art is functional, that it does things, such as teaching us about life, instilling moral values, and persuading us to do certain things. Abrams explains: "The pragmatic orientation, ordering the aim of the artist and the character of the work to the nature, the needs, and the springs of pleasure in the audience, characterized by far the greatest part of criticism from the time of Horace through the eighteenth century" (pp. 20-21).

4. *Expressive theories of art:* These theories focus on the creators of works of art and the creative process, along with the emotional kicks that works of art generate in people. Thus Abrams points out: "Almost all the major critics of the English romantic generation phased definitions or key statements showing a parallel alignment from work to poet. Poetry is the overflow, utterance, or projection of the thought and feelings of the poet; or else (in the chief variant formulation) poetry is defined in terms of the imaginative process which modifies and synthesizes the images, thoughts and feelings of the poet" (pp. 21-22).

There are, then, two sets of opposing theories of art here: (a) the mimetic and the objective and (b) the pragmatic and the emotive. The acronym POEM is a handy mnemonic device for remember-

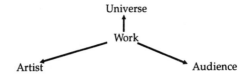

Figure 2.1. Abrams's Framework

TABLE 2.1 Relationships Between Theories and Art

Theory of Art	Elements in Works of Art
mimetic	universe
objective	work
pragmatic	audience
expressive	artist

ing the names of these theories, though MOPE places them in their relationships more accurately: *m*imetic, *o*bjective, *p*ragmatic, and *e*xpressive.

Although Abrams is concerned with literature and theories that focus on literature, we can extend the range and use these four theories to analyze the mass media and interpret the texts carried by the media. We can also see that many of the theories of art developed in recent years can be traced back to these four basic theories. For example, it can be suggested that auteur theory, which focuses on the role of the director in filmmaking, is essentially an expressive theory of art.

Abrams also offers a diagram that, he suggests, shows how these theories relate to one another in an overarching framework (see Figure 2.1). If we line these up against his four theories, we arrive at the set of relationships shown in Table 2.1. If we look at Figure 2.1 and add media to the elements, we move from a triangle to a rectangle, with media in the center, relating to and tied to all four corners of the rectangle. I would suggest we also change the term *universe* to *society*, so we can focus on the relationships that exist among a text, its audience, and society at large. A revision

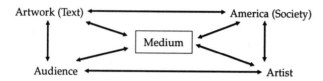

Figure 2.2. Revision of Abrams's Framework

of Abrams's framework is presented in Figure 2.2. This revision enables us to discuss texts in terms of their creators, the media that carry them, their audiences, and society at large. I use alliteration in the figure as a mnemonic device; I am talking about society here, and not America (i.e., the United States) per se.

René Girard, an eminent French literary scholar, has a theory related to mimesis that is of interest here. He argues that Shakespeare's works (and the works of many other authors as well) are informed by what Girard (1991) calls "mimetic desire." People imitate the desire of others and desire things not for their intrinsic qualities, so to speak, but because they are desired by others. This desire or envy is, Girard suggests, a fundamental source of human conflict:

> When we think about those phenomena in which mimicry is likely to play a role, we enumerate such things as dress, mannerisms, facial expressions, speech, stage acting, artistic creation, and so forth, but we never think of desire. Consequently, we see imitation in social life as a force for gregariousness and bland conformity through the mass reproduction of a few social models.
>
> If imitation also plays a role in desire, if it contaminates our urge to acquire and possess, this conventional view, while not entirely false, misses the main point. Imitation does not merely draw people together, it pulls them apart. Paradoxically, it can do these two things simultaneously. Individuals who desire the same thing are united by something so powerful that, so long as they can share whatever they desire, they remain the best of friends; as soon as they cannot, they become the worst of enemies. (p. 3)

Girard touches upon a very interesting notion and suggests that mimesis has more dimensions to it than we might imagine. Not only do texts mirror the world, they also mirror the desires of their characters and, of course, the desires of their readers and audiences. This is not done consciously, of course, but we respond to the mimetic desire in literary works because, so Girard's theory suggests, it mirrors our own hidden thoughts. Girard devotes his book *A Theatre of Envy* (1991) to examining Shakespeare's works and showing how mimetic desire pervades his plays. It is a very interesting, and controversial, use of the concept of mimesis.

Let us move now to the first of the topics in Figure 2.2—artworks, or texts.

Texts

Text, as used here, refers to any work of art. It is a general term for specific works created in various media: novels, plays, films, television shows, short stories, commercials, cartoons, and so on. In the case of a particular television program or a specific film, deciding what the text is poses few problems, but what do we do when we have a serial work of art—a soap opera that stretches over 30 years or a comic strip that, as is true in some cases, has been published for 40 or 50 years? What is the text in such cases—the entire work or some portion of it, such as a complete episode or segment?

Consider the *Dick Tracy* comic strip. This strip went on for many years, but it contained more or less complete segments in which Tracy had to deal with various grotesque villains. These segments were patched together, over the years, with short transitions, so one segment led to the next in rapid succession. There are some texts, such as soap operas, in which such segmentation does not exist; the story lines are all woven together, and there are no discrete beginnings or endings to specific episodes.

There is also the matter of the relations of texts to other texts, a topic I will address in more detail in the discussion of intertextuality. We know that texts often borrow from other texts, sometimes consciously and sometimes unconsciously. What then, we might ask, is the boundary of the text under discussion, and to what degree does its relationship to specific texts, or a series of texts, impinge on its singularity and identity?

In addition, there is the matter of those who "read" the text and their role. Take, for example, a novel. Is the text the work of art, as created by the novelist, or do readers have a role in the creation of the text, as some reader-response theorists (who will be discussed shortly) argue? If a text is not read, is it, like the tree falling in the forest that nobody hears, in some way nonexistent?

Yuri (Jurij) Lotman (1977), a Russian semiotician, writes that "the tendency to interpret *everything* in an artistic text as meaningful is so great that we rightfully consider nothing accidental in a work of art" (p. 17). This would lead to the notion that an artistic text is a work in which everything is important and plays a role, and nothing is accidental. That would explain, in part, why texts are so complex and difficult to interpret. They have their own internal organization, and by using phenomena such as myth and legend, texts function as what Lotman calls "secondary modeling systems," secondary to language itself, which he sees as a primary modeling system.

Art, Lotman suggests, is a "sort of secondary language," and works of art are texts in that language. So for Lotman, texts, as works of art, have the following characteristics:

- very well defined internal organization
- a different kind of language from nontexts, a language that functions beyond the plan of language per se as a secondary language or secondary modeling system
- a multiplanar character, or, in other terms, multiple encoding, which means they are open to being decoded in many different ways

Lotman writes:

Art is the most economical, compact method for storing and transmitting information. But art has other properties wholly worthy of the attention of cyberneticians and perhaps, in time, of design engineers.

Since it can concentrate a tremendous amount of information into the "area" of a very small text (cf. the length of a short story by Chekhov or a psychology textbook) an artistic text manifests yet another feature: it transmits different information to different readers in proportion to each one's comprehension: it provides the reader with a language in which each successive portion of information may be assimilated with repeated readings. It behaves as a kind of living organism which has a feedback channel to the reader and thereby instructs him. (p. 23)

These are the characteristics of the artistic text, what I have referred to above as a "work of art," and they separate it from other kinds of writing and material that are not works of art.

Genres and Texts

As used in contemporary cultural criticism, *genre* refers to a kind of text, with reference, in particular, to mass-mediated texts. Thus, for example, we can talk about a medium, television, the dominant medium of the day, and the genres it carries: commercials, news shows, soap operas, action-adventure programs, situation comedies, sports shows (football, baseball, basketball), interview shows, science fiction shows, how-to-do-it shows (cooking, home repair), spy stories, documentaries, religious shows, and so on. Television also broadcasts many films, which can also be broken down into a number of genres and subgenres as well, such as police stories, science fiction, horror stories, spy stories, comedies (screwball and other kinds), westerns, and action-adventure stories.

In literary studies, the word *genre* is traditionally used somewhat differently, focusing on broader classifications, such as histories, comedies, and tragedies. Genre fiction, films, and other works are often described as subliterary, formulaic works that are created for the so-called lowest common denominator, or the largest number of people possible. The theory suggests that the lower the taste level in the text, the larger the number of people it will appeal to. Although this may be true of certain kinds of works at the extremes (such as romance novels), it is not true of other genre works, such as mysteries by Dashiell Hammett and Raymond Chandler.

We talk about genres because of our need to classify things, which we do to get a sense of how texts relate to one another and to gain some perspective on them. There is an interesting philosophical issue related to genres, namely, whether or not "classes" of things exist and what their ontological status is. Is a genre (a classification) as real as a text (a particular work)? The way we classify things determines the information we obtain, so it may be that in using genres to differentiate, for example, between so-called serious literature and genre literature, we do a disservice to much genre literature. There may be other ways of looking at what we classify as genre texts that is more useful.

Is a text such as *Blade Runner,* which features a detective searching for renegade androids, or replicants, to be seen as a detective film or a science fiction film? In many cases, it is difficult to say which genre is dominant. And if we decide that a film, such as *Blade Runner* or one of Charlie Chaplin's comedies, is a great work of art, or perhaps even a classic, does the film suddenly lose its genre identity and become something else?

Genre can be distinguished from formula, though some critics use the terms interchangeably. *Genre* refers to a kind of text, such as a detective story, whereas *formula* relates to the use of certain conventions (relative to time, location, kinds of heroes and heroines, villains, plots, themes, weapons, and so on) found in the text. Thus, for example, in the detective story genre, we have a number of different formulas—including the classical detective story, the tough-guy detective story, and the procedural detective story—all of which focus on different things, but all of which involve the attempt to find out who the criminal (nowadays, usually the murderer) is.

Interpretation of Texts

Literary theorists make a distinction between analysis and interpretation. *Analysis* involves, in essence, taking a literary work apart and seeing how the parts fit together. The so-called New Criticism of the 1940s and 1950s in the United States, as repre-

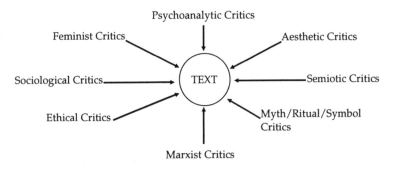

Figure 2.3. Critical Domains

sented by the work of Robert Penn Warren and Cleanth Brooks, was, from this perspective, analytic. Brooks and Warren analyzed (today we might say *deconstructed*) a poem such as Joyce Kilmer's "Trees" and showed that the bits and pieces of the poem did not form a logical whole.

Interpretation, as I will use the term, involves the application of concepts attached to some intellectual domain—such as psychoanalytic thought, semiotic theory, Marxist thought, sociological theory, anthropological theory, or feminist thought—to some text. This can be illustrated as in Figure 2.3; visualize a text, like a piece of sculpture, surrounded by different domains, all of which throw light on the text from their own particular perspectives. Some critics may apply a number of different interpretive methods in combination. Thus there are semiotically inclined Marx- ist critics; critics who combine semiotics and psychoanalytic thought; critics who view texts from the perspectives of psychoanalytic thought and Marxism; critics who combine psychoanalytic thought, semiotics, and feminism; and so on.

Literary texts, like all forms of artistic expression, are enormously complicated. Critics do not just criticize out of the blue; they usually belong to particular groups, adhere to particular philosophies, and have associations with particular disciplines, and their criticisms are connected to their groups, disciplines, and belief systems. Criticism always comes from a point of view. It is

TABLE 2.2 Critical Perspectives

semiotic	psychoanalytic	Marxist
feminist	mythical/symbolic	archetypal
sociological	historical	biographical
aesthetic	ethical	rhetorical

not objective, though most critics believe that their own perspectives are the ones that are best suited for the texts they deal with.

Table 2.2 lists a number of different perspectives in three columns. It is possible to use one, two, or three (and maybe more) of these perspectives in interpreting a text, and to move across the columns or up and down them, or both across and up and down the columns. The possibilities, as you can see, are considerable. All of these perspectives are discussed in this book, in one place or another.

One question that suggests itself when we counter disagreements about a theory or a text is, Who is right? Each critic would argue that his or her mode of interpretation is best in that it deals most completely with the important aspects of the text. There is no way to be sure, which is why there can be an endless number of articles and books on a single text, such as *Hamlet*. Texts are finite, but interpretations of texts replicate in geometrical progression.

Hermeneutics

Hermeneutics concerns the methodology of literary interpretation. Originally, it involved interpretation, or exegesis, of the Scriptures. The word *hermeneutics* comes from the Greek *hermeneuticos,* which refers to someone skilled in interpretation or in making things clear. The Greek word is connected to Hermes, the messenger of the gods, the god of invention and roads, who was known to be cunning, inventive, and a thief. The contemporary practitioners of hermeneutics are also cunning and inventive, but relatively few of them are thieves.

In contemporary literary and cultural criticism, hermeneutics is an approach to uncovering the meaning of a text (or cultural activity, which can be seen as being like a text) not by cerebration or objective intellectual analysis, but by entering into the text. The text is considered a self-contained universe, so to speak, and the hermeneutical critic wishes to experience this universe rather than "know" it through intellectual operations.

In a celebrated and often-reproduced passage, the French critic Georges Poulet describes the aim of the hermeneutical critic:

> Like everyone, I believe that the end of criticism is to arrive at an intimate knowledge of critical reality. However, it seems to me that such an intimacy is only possible to the extent that critical thought *becomes* the thought criticized, which it can succeed in doing only by re-feeling, re-thinking, re-imagining this thought from the inside. Nothing could be less objective than such a movement of mind. Contrary to what one might expect, criticism must prevent itself from seeing some sort of *object* (whether it is the person of the author seen as an Other, or his work considered as a Thing); for what must be arrived at is a *subject*, which is to say a spiritual activity that one cannot understand except by putting oneself in its place and causing it to play again within us its role as subject. (quoted in Scholes, 1974, p. 7)

Thus literary texts are not analyzed. Instead, they are "recovered" as the critic enters into the work and experiences it imaginatively, rather than remaining outside it and seeing it as an object to be studied.

The focus in hermeneutics remains on the text, of course. In this respect it differs from reception theory, which focuses on the role played by the reader of the text, and not on the alleged "meaning" contained in the text. Hermeneutics also differs from structural analysis, which tends to treat the text as an object to be analyzed, to see how meaning is produced and effects are generated, and from Marxist approaches, which consider matters such as the production of texts and social and economic forces at work in the societies in which the texts are produced.

Implicit in this discussion is the notion that a text does not have only one valid interpretation. A critic, as I have noted, always has a point of view, a domain to which he or she is attached, a disciplinary perspective, a social or political group with which he or she identifies (Marxist, feminist, Catholic, Freudian, ad infinitum), and it is important to keep this in mind. Critics are also subject to social and political influences, fashions (intellectual and other), trends, and the like. *Rashomon*, the brilliant film in which everyone involved in a rape and death has a different story to tell, is the metaphor. We no longer believe that texts have only one meaning and always have the same effects on audiences (the hypodermic theory of communication). Though it is difficult for some people to understand, texts can be interpreted from many different perspectives.

The question, that arises then, is, Whose interpretation is most revealing, most interesting? Whose interpretation deals with more elements of the text, reveals most about the characters involved, and sheds most light on the relevance of the text to society and culture? And how do we find the answers to these questions? That is one of the enigmas of criticism.

Reception Theory

Reception theory has been developed by theorists such as Hans Robert Jauss and Wolfgang Iser, both of whom are professors at the University of Constance in Germany. An interesting parallel can be drawn between uses and gratifications theory and reception theory. Some mass media theorists have developed the notion of uses and gratifications, which focuses not on the effects of mass media on people, but on the way people use the media and the gratifications they get from the media. Reception theorists are vaguely similar in that they focus on the roles that audiences (readers of texts, decoders of texts) play in the scheme of things, and not on texts themselves. As Iser (1972/1988) has written:

The phenomenological theory of art lays full stress on the idea that, in considering a literary work, one must take into account not only the actual text but also, and in equal measure, the actions involved in responding to that text. Thus Roman Ingarden confronts the structure of the literary text with the ways in which it can be *konkretisiert* (realized). The text as such offers different "schematized views" through which the subject matter of the work can come to light, but the actual bringing to light is an action of *Konkretisation*. (p. 212)

What this suggests, then, is that audiences—and in the case of a specific work, such as a novel, readers—play an important role in what we might call the "realization" of a text.

Iser makes a distinction between two polarities: One is the artistic, which refers to the work created by the author, and the other is the aesthetic, which refers to realization, which is done by the reader. He explains this notion as follows:

If this is so, then the literary work has two poles, which we might call the artistic, and the aesthetic: the artistic refers to the text created by the author and the aesthetic to the aesthetic realization accomplished by the reader. From this polarity it follows that the literary work cannot be completely identical with the text, or with the realization of the text, but in fact must lie halfway between the two. The work is more than the text, for the text only takes on life when it is realized, and furthermore the realization is by no means independent of the individual disposition of the reader—though this in turn is acted upon by the different patterns of the text. (p. 212)

Literary works, in a sense, do not exist until they are realized by a reader. (One thinks of Berkeley's famous dictum, "To be is to be perceived.") Texts have a virtual or immanent reality that is not actualized until some reader (or audience) reads or sees or hears the text.

Ingarden (1968) argues, if you push things far enough, that the reader has an equal measure of importance in realizing texts. Thus the world is turned topsy-turvy as far as our ideas about authorship are concerned, for texts no longer stand on their own, and artists and authors, those who bring texts into being, no longer

TABLE 2.3 Relations Between Text and Reader

Text	(Work)	Reader
author		reader, audience
artistic plane		aesthetic plane
sender		receiver
creates a text		realizes the text
text a system of signs to be understood		text a site for creation of meanings

can claim sole possession, so to speak, of their texts. If we were to translate this notion into communication theory terms it would be that the receiver now has become equal to, or equally as important as, the sender of the message. These ideas are displayed in Table 2.3.

Reception theory argues that we must not privilege, or give undue importance to, the text, and that we must take into account "the role of the reader" (Eco, 1984) and the way different readers (or viewers, in the case of visual media) interpret texts. Texts, in a sense, do not exist, but rather are entities that can be brought into being only by readers. Many authors do not like the notion that their works, like Cinderella, can be awakened only by the kiss of a reader/Prince Charming, but Iser and other reception theorists do have a point.

Deconstruction

It is extremely difficult to say what deconstruction is and is not, in part because it is quite difficult to understand the ideas of one of the founders of this perspective/school/philosophy, Jacques Derrida, and of other critics who write from this perspective. What deconstruction argues, it seems, as an overriding theme, is that texts do not have determinate meanings, and that a close examination of any text shows this to be so.

In a sense, as in reception theory, readers can be said to create the meanings of the texts they read and works of art they examine. One problem with this strategy of textual interpretation is that it can lead to extremes. A text may not have only one "real" meaning, but that does not suggest that anything goes and that any interpretation of a text or work of art is as good as any other.

The basis for the deconstructionist approach to reading texts is philosophical. The belief that there is a "right" way to read a text comes from our philosophy and, in particular, the work of Ferdinand de Saussure (1966), who suggests that there is a system (essentially of linguistic oppositions) underlying the various different works of art and literature we see about us, in a domain (language) external to these works. The structuralists, who are influenced by Saussure's theory of language (and the notion that meaning stems from oppositions), show that there are underlying sets of oppositions that give meaning to texts. Deconstructionists argue that there is usually something wrong with the system of oppositions and relationships that structuralists find in texts and that the logic of a text, as a system of signs, inevitably tends to "betray" itself, so the whole structural edifice comes tumbling down.

According to Derrida, whose work has led to the poststructuralist movement, there is no "center" or system of ideas outside of the text that enables us to understand them and interpret them in one way. An important literary theorist, Hillis Miller, explains deconstruction as follows:

> Deconstruction as a mode of interpretation works by a careful and circumspect entering of each textual labyrinth. . . . The deconstructive critic seeks to find, by this process of retracing, the element in the system which is alogical, the thread in the text in question which will unravel it all, or the loose stone which will pull down the whole building. The deconstruction, rather, annihilates the ground on which the building stands by showing that the text has already annihilated that ground, knowingly or unknowingly. Deconstruction is not a dismantling of the structure of the text but a demonstration that it has already dismantled itself. (quoted in Abrams, 1989, p. 560)

One problem with all this, as critics such as Abrams have pointed out, is that deconstruction is a "fail-safe" enterprise; there is no way to test its validity.

Deconstruction leads to ingenious and fascinating interpretations of texts and brilliant exhibitions of intellectual dexterity, but it
is, some have suggested, ultimately unsatisfying. And deconstruction does not take into account, as Abrams has argued, the way
we experience texts, the sense we have that they are unique, or
the way they excite us, generating feelings and passions in people; others have argued that deconstruction fails to address the
social and political dimensions of texts.

Deconstruction is a difficult concept to explain, and now some
critics suggest that deconstruction is passé, and the study of literature and culture has moved to a post-poststructuralist and post-
theory age, as a repudiation of deconstruction and other similar
theories of literature. (One nice thing about literary theory and
cultural studies is that they are always in the process of change,
and theories and theorists come and go with ever-increasing rapid-
ity.) The most important new theory in these areas is postmodernism. Let me jump from the frying pan of deconstruction into
the fire of postmodernism, which is also the subject of a great deal
of controversy.

Postmodernism

People use the term *postmodernism* in so many different ways
that it has been rendered meaningless, some say, having become all
things to all men and women. (Some argue that postmodernism
is, like deconstruction, passé and that we have moved into an era
of post-postmodernism.) Although it is difficult to define postmodernism, there are certain ideas that generally have been associated with it. I will discuss these in an effort to give some kind of
meaning to the term.

The term *postmodernism* suggests that our culture has moved
into a new phase, beyond that called modernism. So, at the very
least, we have to know what modernism is to know what postmodernism is not. *Modernism* refers to the period that came into
being as a result of the Renaissance, which was a movement that

was connected with the rise of individualism and the beginnings of the capitalist, bureaucratic industrial order. In the realm of the arts and culture, modernism is associated with the writings of authors such as James Joyce, Franz Kafka, Marcel Proust, Robert Musil, Thomas Mann, William Faulkner, T. S. Eliot, and Luigi Pirandello. In the visual arts, modernism refers to the work of artists such as Pablo Picasso, Henri Matisse, and Georges Braque, and movements such as futurism, dadaism, and surrealism. In music, modernism is associated with the work of composers such as Igor Stravinsky, Arnold Schoenberg, and Béla Bartók. These creative artists and the modernist movement reflected major changes in the expressive arts. According to Mike Featherstone (1988),

> The basic features of modernism can be summarized as: an aesthetic self-consciousness and reflexiveness; a rejection of narrative structure in favor of simultaneity and montage; an exploration of the para-doxical, ambiguous and uncertain open-ended nature of reality; and a rejection of the notion of the integrated personality in favor of an emphasis on the destructured, dehumanized subject. (p. 202)

Featherstone points out that some of the features of modern-ism in the arts have been appropriated by postmodern artists, so it is not easy to distinguish the two movements in some cases. He lists some of the features connected with postmodernism in the arts:

> the effacement of the boundary between art and everyday life; the collapse of the hierarchical distinction between high and mass/ popular culture; a stylistic promiscuity favouring eclecticism and the mixing of codes; parody, pastiche, irony, playfulness and the celebration of the surface "depthlessness" of culture; the decline of the originality/genius of the artistic producer and the assumption that art can only be repetitious. (p. 203)

Featherstone adds that one can discuss modernism and post-modernism in broader perspectives than the arts, involving the whole of culture and the relationship that exists between it and the economic order and the political order.

Todd Gitlin (1989) offers a slightly different perspective on postmodernism:

> It self-consciously splices genres, attitudes, styles. It relishes the blur-
> ring or juxtaposition of forms (fiction-nonfiction), stances (straight-
> ironic), moods (violent-comic), cultural levels (high-low). . . . It pulls
> the rug out from under itself, displaying an acute self-consciousness
> about the work's constructed nature. It takes pleasure in the play
> of surfaces, and derides the search for depth as mere nostalgia.
> (p. 52)

This gives us a sense of what postmodernism is, but Gitlin does not stop there. He provides a long list of examples of postmod-ernism in our culture, suggesting the degree to which Americans, perhaps more than any other people, are living in a postmodern society:

> One postmodernist trope is the list, as if culture were a garage sale,
> so it is appropriate to evoke post-modernism by offering a list of
> examples, for better and for worse: Michael Graves' Portland Build-
> ing, Philip Johnson's AT&T, and hundreds of more or less skillful
> derivatives; Robert Rauschenberg's silk screens; Andy Warhol's
> multiple-image paintings, photo-realism, Larry Rivers erasures
> and pseudo-pageantry, Sherrie Levine's photographs of "classic"
> photographs; Disneyland, Las Vegas, suburban strips, shopping
> malls, mirror-glass office building facades; William Burroughs,
> Tom Wolfe, Donald Barthelme, Monty Python, Don DeLillo, Joe Isuzu
> "He's Lying" commercials, Philip Glass, *Star Wars*, Spalding Gray,
> David Hockney . . . Max Headroom, David Byrne, Twyla Tharp
> (choreographing Beach Boys and Frank Sinatra songs), Italo Calvino.
> (Gitlin, 1989, pp. 52-53)

The list continues, at considerable length. What I have quoted sug-gests the degree to which our culture, our consciousness, and our psyches have been shaped, so it is suggested, by postmodernism.

It is interesting to note that the theory of postmodernism has been elaborated by French thinkers such as Jean Baudrillard, Jacques Derrida, Michel Foucault, Jacques Lacan, and Jean-François Lyotard. Cultural criticism in the United States is based largely on the work of these authors and a few others, such as Louis Althusser, Roland Barthes, Claude Lévi-Strauss, and some other European thinkers, mostly Russian and German, thrown in for good measure.

We Americans, so we are to understand, without realizing what we were doing, created a quintessentially postmodern society, and now we have the French (and others) explaining to us what we have done in theoretical terms and U.S. cultural analysts explaining the French theorists to us and offering lists of works of art and aspects of our culture that are postmodern, so we can recognize the extent to which we have become postmodernized.

Feminist Criticism

In the past 30 years or so, a form of criticism that focuses upon feminist issues has evolved and is now an important approach to texts and cultural analysis in general. At the most obvious level, feminist criticism is concerned with matters related to gender. For example, some critics study the way women have been characterized in the media and deal with such things as the numbers of women (compared with the numbers of men) in mass-mediated texts, the role of women in dramatic texts, the sexual exploitation of women's bodies and the related matter of the male gaze in texts, the values and beliefs in genres that are directed primarily toward women (such as romance novels and soap operas), and how women are represented in these genres. We can summarize these and related considerations by saying they focus on the following:

- *roles* women have in texts and, by extension, everyday life
- *exploitation* of women as sex objects
- *domination by men* in the workplace, sexual relationships, and other areas of life
- *the consciousness of women* as it relates to their lives

A number of feminist theorists have argued that many societies are patriarchal, in that they revolve around male power (and, in particular, male phallic power) and masculine ways of seeing the world, conducting science, and so on. These theorists argue that content analyses of women's roles in the media do not go far enough, for they do not offer women a philosophical stance, a means of dealing with their domination and exploitation. Kathryn Cirksena (1987) offers a succinct summary of feminist concerns relative to communication studies (and by extension cultural studies):

> Three facets of a radical feminist critique that I consider pertinent to communication processes include: the social construction of knowledge and information, especially those assumptions concerning gender; the role of language in supporting gender-based inequalities; and conceptions of "difference" as they challenge masculinist philosophers' assertions about the universality of the human condition and related methodological and political positions. (p. 19)

Some feminist critics attack the alleged objectivity of traditional social science research and the production of knowledge in the social sciences, arguing that it is biased and does not take into account the subjective experiences of women. This raises an interesting issue: Is there an objective way of studying society and culture, based on social science techniques, or is there an alternative way of doing this that attacks notions such as distance and objectivity and gives more attention to subjective matters? And is objectivity "male" and is subjectivity "female"? Many feminist critics argue that social science methodologies are masculinist and biased in various ways toward male perspectives, a situation that leads, ultimately, to the maintenance of the status quo and the domination of women by men.

Many feminist critics argue that they are concerned with inequality, but is this concept male or female? And, by extension, we must ask whether all concepts are gender specific or, at least, have implications as far as the social, economic, cultural, and, most particularly, sexual relationships that exist between men and women are concerned. This leads to our next subject, phallocentric theory, which can be seen as an adjunct of feminist theory.

Phallocentric Theory

The notion that societies are male dominated and, even more directly, reflect the power of the male phallus is a central notion of much feminist thought. According to this idea, the institutions of societies, the cultures found in societies, the roles assigned to women in the elite arts, in the mass media, in every aspect of life, are shaped (to a certain degree unconsciously) by male power, male sexuality in general, and, in particular, by the male phallus.

Males, according to this theory, take the power relationships that exist in society as natural; they are, therefore, blind to its existence and react to suggestions that our society is phallocentric with ridicule. Jane Gaines (1987) discusses the way feminist critics developed a theory linking male spectators and Freud's theories of voyeurism and fetishism:

> In the United States, one of the earliest attempts to theorize the eroticized female image, Maureen Turin's "Gentlemen Consume Blondes," analyzes *Gentlemen Prefer Blondes* in Marxist terms of commodity exchange. Although men are implicated in the title, Turin makes no gender distinctions in her discussion of the way cinema makes voyeurs and fetishists of us all while at the same time excusing our tendencies. Soon after, Lucy Fisher, in her examination of Busby Berkeley's decorative uses of the showgirl, made a tentative connection between fetishism and male, as opposed to female, eroticism. The *Cahiers de Cinema* analysis of Marlene Dietrich in *Morocco* . . . assumes a phallocentric society and is interested in both the economic and the erotic functions of the fetish. (p. 359)

We see that the notion that we live in a phallocentric society, in which men's sexuality and power are dominant, can be understood in both Freudian and Marxist terms. (And Gaines points out that it is the male spectator who must be the focus of analysis.)

Gaines adds that the Marxist notion of commodity fetishism, which gives "magical qualities" to the fetish, has not been developed, whereas the Freudian concept of fetishism, tied to sexuality, has been used extensively by feminist critics. But there are ideological implications to psychoanalytic approaches to media, as she explains:

> Recent psychoanalytic theory hypothesizes that all conventional language and pictorial representation is male-biased, for reasons rooted in the psychology of infantile sexuality. To understand the dominant cinema as thoroughly voyeuristic and to identify all sexual representation of women with it as phallic substitution implies a definite political analysis. If even everyday viewing is organized along these lines, with patriarchal power relations being reproduced in every depiction of women on a magazine page or billboard, then we are all ideological captives. (pp. 359-360)

This notion that all imagery is naturally male and thereby reinforces patriarchal relationships in phallocentric societies is, it must be pointed out, a questionable one. Some feminist critics argue that female images are possible, and other critics dispute the notion that language and pictorial representation are naturally male.

We turn now to our next subject area, formalist perspectives on texts and related topics such as defamiliarization, which focus not on the social and political dimensions of works but on the devices and other elements found in works that help them function as works of art.

Formalism

In 1915 and 1916, two groups of Russian literary critics developed an approach to literature (and, by extension, other arts) known as formalism. Rather than considering the messages carried by literature about politics and society, for example, these theorists focused their attention on how literature works, on "literaryness" and what it is that separates literature from other things (such as everyday speech and ordinary language, or other art forms).

Their approach was mechanistic; they looked for the *devices* (a term they used) in literary works that make them function as literature. Their concern, then, was with the formal properties of literary works instead of the content of these works (reflections of society, its values and beliefs, and so on). They argued that many of the things that traditional critics had focused on—figurative language, symbols, images—are found in everyday language use, so it did not make sense to focus on these phenomena, in that they were both literary and extraliterary.

One of the more important formalist critics, Viktor Shklovsky, developed the notion that literature and the arts, in general, must "make strange" (*ostraneni* in Russian) and "defamiliarize" people from their accustomed perceptions of things and help us see things from new perspectives. Another notion the formalists believed in was that one way literature functioned was to call attention to itself and its devices, instead of hiding them. Here they anticipated the theories of Bertolt Brecht, who believed that art must "alienate" people, what is called "the estrangement effect" (*Verfremdung*), and call attention to itself and the institutions of society that are historical and not natural, and therefore able to be changed. This differed radically from the notion held by some critics that in literature and theater, for example, there occurs, and should occur, a "willing suspension of disbelief."

Fredric Jameson (1972) explains the significance of the formalist approach:

> The originality of the Formalist's idea of technique is to be found in its inversion. For Aristotle and the neo-Aristotelians, everything in the work of art exists for some ultimate purpose, which is the characteristic emotion or peculiar pleasure of the work itself as an object consumed. For the Formalists everything in the work exists in order to permit the work to come into being in the first place. The advantage of this approach is that whereas ultimately the Aristotelian analyses end up outside the work (in psychology and the extra-literary problems of the conventionality of emotion), for Shklovsky such emotions as pity and fear are themselves to be considered constituent parts or element of the work in the first place. (p. 82)

He adds, discussing the functions of formalist theory and relating them to a theory we have already discussed, mimesis: "Its intent is to suspend the common-sense view of the work of art as mimesis (i.e. possessing content) and as source and purveyor of emotion" (p. 83).

Ultimately, as Jameson points out in a discussion of the work of several formalist theorists, what they threw out the front door (psychological, philosophical, and biographical matters) they took in by the back door, but that is another matter. What is important to remember about the formalists is that they focused on the form of literary works, not on their content, and on the devices used by writers that made a work literature rather than something else. For the formalists, the relationship of elements in a text were basic and of fundamental interest, not the social, political, or psychological "content" of a work. Ultimately, their ideas suggest that works can be differentiated in terms of their formal elements and thus categorized according to genres. We can, of course, apply the insights of the formalists to all kinds of expressive arts—that is, elite culture and popular culture—and other aspects of culture as well.

Defamiliarization

As mentioned above, the concept of defamiliarization was elaborated by the Russian literary theorist Viktor Shklovsky (1989), who wrote, "As perception becomes habitual, it becomes automatic." One of the most important functions of art, for Shklovsky, is to shock us, so to speak, so that we no longer are victims of habit. Works of art help us to recover excitement about life and to see familiar things in new ways.

> Art exists to help us recover the sensation of life; it exists to make us feel things, to make the stone *stony*. The end of art is to give a sensation of the object as seen, not as recognized. The technique of art is to make things "unfamiliar," to make forms obscure, so as to increase the difficulty and the duration of perception. The act of perception in art is an end in itself and must be prolonged. *In art, it is our experience of the process of construction that counts, not the final product.* (Shklovsky, quoted in Scholes, 1974, pp. 83-84)

As Scholes (1974) points out, defamiliarization techniques themselves become conventions. In literature, for example, we see this in the creation of point of view, style, and plot, which start off as agents of defamiliarization and become, eventually, conventions. The writer ends up, ultimately, having to create new techniques of defamiliarization—techniques that expose the old techniques to ridicule and, ultimately, parody.

It might be suggested that one of the differences between "elite" arts and popular arts is that the latter tend to be much more conventional and formulaic and are not particularly interested in defamiliarization processes, which might cause problems for audiences. One way popular audiences "recognize" what is going on in texts is by knowing the formulas and conventions used in these texts; another way is by seeing resemblances between and among texts. This leads to the subject of textual autonomy, and to an examination of the work of one of the most important contemporary Russian literary theorists and critics, Mikhail Bakhtin.

Dialogical Theory

Bakhtin has argued that communication is essentially "dialogical." When we write or speak, according to this theory, we always do so with an audience in mind, and our writing or speech is always connected to ideas and thoughts that have been communicated in the past. Thus the concept of dialogue is given importance and, it is argued, is a more useful and correct way of understanding communication than monologue, which gives primacy to the person doing the writing and thinking.

What we say, for example, is intimately connected to the person or persons we are talking to and to the responses we can expect (and this dialogic process goes on even if we are not actually talking to persons; it occurs whenever we write or, by extension, do any kind of creative activity). There are two important phenomena to keep in mind, then. First, there is the past, which has an impact on our ideas and what we create. Second, there is the future and the responses we anticipate from our audience (real or imagined), which affect what we do. As Bakhtin (1981) has written:

> Every extra-artistic prose discourse—in any of its forms, quotidian, rhetorical, scholarly—cannot fail to be oriented toward the "already uttered," the "already known," the "common opinion" and so forth. The dialogic orientation of discourse is a phenomenon that is, of course, a property of *any* discourse. . . .
>
> . . . every word is directed toward an *answer* and cannot escape the profound influence of the answering word that it anticipates. The word in living conversation is directly, blatantly, oriented toward a future answer-word: it provokes an answer, anticipates it and structures itself in the answer's direction. Forming itself in the atmosphere of the already spoken, the word is at the same time determined by that which has not yet been said but which is needed and in fact anticipated by the answering word. Such is the situation in any living dialogue. (pp. 279-280)

Thus Bakhtin argues that the analogy we should make to understand communication—and, in particular, the creation of texts—is that of dialogue and not monologue. Conversation, not monologism (or talking to oneself) is the basic metaphor.

Texts, then, are suspended between the past and the future. They are intertextual (a concept that will be discussed in more detail in Chapter 4) in that they are affected, to varying degrees, by texts that have preceded them and have, to varying degrees, affected their creators, and, at the same time, they also anticipate the future. This concept, dialogism, gives us new insights into the creative process and into the role the audience plays in communication, whether it be conversation or the creation of artistic texts.

It also points out how important the cultural context is for creators, because the creators of artistic texts, whether they realize it or not, are profoundly affected by the social and cultural milieux in which they find themselves and by the texts and other creative works that already exist and that cast a shadow on, or provide a frame of reference (when not providing models) for, all works being created at a given moment.

Montage and Meaning

I conclude this discussion of literary (and aesthetic) theory with the work of one more Russian thinker, Sergei Eisenstein, who was a brilliant film director in addition to being an important aesthetician and theorist. Eisenstein is the person most commonly associated with the theory of montage (*montage* means, literally, assembling). He notes:

> Even the most fanatical opponent of montage will agree that it is not merely because the film strip at our disposal is not of infinite length, and consequently, being condemned to working with pieces of restricted lengths, we have to stick one piece of it on to another occasionally.
>
> The "leftists" of montage saw it from the opposite extreme. While playing with pieces of film, they discovered a certain property in the toy which kept them astonished for years. This property consisted in the fact *that two pieces of film of any kind, placed together, inevitably combine into a new concept, a new quality, arising out of that juxtaposition.* (Eisenstein, 1947, p. 4)

Eisenstein also describes montage as a "series of connecting shocks arranged in a certain sequence and directed at the audience" for the purpose of generating a desired reaction—an analogy that calls to mind Pavlov's experiments with dogs (Wollen, 1973, p. 39).

It is sequence that generates meaning—a single picture or shot by itself has no meaning, or is ambiguous. It is when a shot is combined with other shots in a sequence that we find meaning in a film. As one of Eisenstein's experiments demonstrates, the emotion on a person's face in a given shot is determined by the shots that come before and after. Thus, for example, we may see a single shot of a man with tears rolling down his face. If the shots before and after this shot have a humorous content, we interpret the shot of the man with tears as laughing; if the shots before and after this shot have a tragic content, we interpret the shot as showing the man crying. We are very close here to Saussure's argument that concepts mean nothing in themselves, but take their meaning only differentially.

Eisenstein also makes another important point relative to montage:

> The strength of montage resides in this, that it includes in the creative process the emotions and mind of the spectator. The spectator is compelled to proceed along that selfsame creative road that the author travelled in creating the image. The spectator not only sees the represented elements of the finished work, but also experiences the dynamic process of the emergence and assembly of the image just as it was experienced by the author. (p. 32)

That is, the montage is not to be seen primarily as a representation of something, but as a series of images that lead to the creation, in the mind of the filmmaker and in the minds of spectators, of a certain idea or feeling or emotion, and this is very powerful and exciting.

Conclusion

In this chapter I have dealt with a number of the most important topics and concepts found in literary (and, by extension, aesthetic) theory. These concepts are valuable because they help us make sense of texts; literary theory is not an arid form of scholasticism, speculating about the number of angels that can exist on the head of a pin. Rather, literary theory raises important issues about texts, readers and audiences of texts, and the relations of works of art to culture and of cultural matters to society and politics.

Cultural criticism is not just about art and literature, but about the role that culture, in both aesthetic and anthropological senses, plays in the scheme of things—a role that we now see is increasingly important not only for what it reveals about our social, economic, and political institutions, but also for how it shapes these institutions and our consciousness. Culture, we now recognize, has consequences.

Karl Marx

3

Marxism and Cultural Criticism

Before I begin this discussion of Marxist theory, I should point out that Marxism is not monolithic, and neither is Marxist criticism. There are a number of different schools of Marxist critics, and all of them base their criticism on varying and sometimes conflicting interpretations of Marx's theories and how they can be applied to analyzing culture in general and, more specifically, literary texts, works of elite culture, popular culture, and the mass media.

Even though Marxism generally has been discredited as an economic theory and as a political philosophy (as recent events in Eastern Europe and what used to be called the Soviet Union suggest), Marxism still informs the work and dominates the thinking of large numbers of cultural critics—especially European ones, who have influenced or shaped the thinking of critics elsewhere. Many Marxist critics do not believe that there should be a violent overthrow of the political system in their countries. These Marxists use Marx's philosophical beliefs and concepts to attack the ills they find (or claim to find) in so-called bourgeois capitalist societies.

In the Soviet Union and its satellites, before the fall of communism, there were debates about how to apply Marxist theories to culture. Hard-line Marxists endorsed an aesthetic of "socialist realism" (a perverse combination of the mimetic and pragmatic theories of art) and attacked creative artists they felt were not realists. Liberal Marxists were more open to experimental work, to modernist artists and writers such as Pablo Picasso, Franz Kafka, and James Joyce. So Marxist criticism was never monolithic, and neither was Marxism. And, some argue, neither was the thinking of Karl Marx, which, they suggest, evolved over the years.

Base/Superstructure

In Marxist thought, the base (the mode of production, the system of economic relations found in a given society) shapes the super-structure (the institutions in that society, such as the church, the education system, the art world, and the legal system). The base does not determine the superstructure; if it did, every society that reaches a certain level of development would have a super-structure—cultural and social arrangements—more or less identical to that of other societies.

Friedrich Engels, who collaborated with Marx on a number of works, gives more importance to economic considerations than some Marxists believe they merit. According to Engels (1972):

> The new facts made imperative a new examination of all past history. Then it was seen that *all* past history, with the exception of its primitive stages, was the history of class struggles; that these warring classes of society are always the products of the modes of production and of exchange; in a word, of the *economic* conditions of their time; that the economic structure of society always furnishes the real basis, starting from which we can alone work out the ultimate explanation of the whole superstructure of juridical and political institutions as well as of the religious, philosophical, and other ideas of a given historical period. (p. 621)

Economic institutions, the base, are fundamental and necessary to keep in mind, but not sufficient to explain the way institutions develop in society and how they affect groups and individuals. The above statement by Engels is somewhat ambiguous; "the real basis, starting from which we can alone work out" can be read as meaning that it is sufficient, or its opposite.

The notion that economic relations alone *determine* the way a society evolves and the character of its institutions is commonly known as vulgar Marxism. It is too simplistic and reductionistic and does not take human agency into consideration. Consciousness may be socially produced, Marxists argue, but it is always filtered through the minds of men and women who are active in the world and whose personalities and experiences also shape their conceptions.

The Frankfurt School of Criticism

One group of Marxist critics, known as the Frankfurt school, flourished in Germany in the 1930s and in the United States in the 1940s (and for some decades after, because many of the members of the Frankfurt school came to the United States to teach). Members of this school, such as Theodor W. Adorno, Herbert Marcuse, and Max Horkheimer, focused their attention on what might be described as problems of the superstructure. They argued that the mass media had, in effect, prevented history from working out the way it should have, in Marxist terms, by subverting the masses. According to these members of the Frankfurt school, people in the working classes—that is, the masses—became involved in consumer culture and the mindless entertainments offered by popular culture and, brainwashed by the mass media, forgot about their class identities and the need for revolution, or, at least, the need for major structural (economic and political) changes in their societies. Adorno's writings contain many of the criticisms typically made by these philosophers. He attacks mass culture as follows:

> Rigid institutionalization transforms modern mass culture into a medium of undreamed of psychological control. The repetitiveness, the selfsameness, and the ubiquity of modern mass culture tend of make for automatized reactions and to weaken the forces

of individual resistance. . . . The increasing strength of modern mass culture is further enhanced by changes in the sociological structure of the audience. The old cultured elite does not exist any more; the modern intelligentsia only partially corresponds to it. At the same time, huge strata of the population formerly unacquainted with art have become cultural "consumers." (Adorno, 1957, p. 476)

The message of mass culture, Adorno continues, is a hidden one of conformity and adjustment, "identification with the status quo" that becomes a pattern of response in individuals.

Maintaining the status quo, Marxists argue, is very important for the ruling classes in capitalist societies, who want to keep control of all realms and like things just the way they are. Members of the masses, Adorno asserts, not only lose the ability to see reality as it is, because they have been exposed to so much stereotyping and to an atmosphere in which crime is seen as normal, they even lose the capacity for life experience.

According to Adorno (1948), people who attend concerts are also victims, although they do not recognize it; they indulge in empty ritual when they are fed light, easy-to-appreciate music:

Sacrosanct traditional music has come to resemble commercial mass production in the character of its performances and in its role in the life of the listener and its substance has not escaped this influence. Music is inextricably bound up with what Clement Greenberg called the division of all art into kitsch and the avant-garde, and this kitsch—with its dictate of profit over culture—has long since conquered the social sphere. (p. 10)

Thus even people who attend concerts of classical music, who think they appreciate what we would describe as "elite" culture, are only fooling themselves, because their tastes have been debased just like everyone else's.

This elitism found in the works of Adorno and other members of the Frankfurt school may be connected to their own sense of status loss; they had come from a hierarchical society in Germany, where they were members of the elite class, to a more egalitarian society in the United States, and they did not like the way they were treated or the culture in which they found themselves. There was a kind of irony in the position of the Frankfurt school, for the very freedom and openness its members found in U.S. society were the instruments, so their argument went, of its domination and repression.

The notion that culture and the arts are ideological tools of ruling elites who use them to brainwash the masses is very close to the Stalinist theory known as *zhdanovism*. This theory argued that works of art should be characterized by "socialist realism"— heroic truck drivers giving apples to rosy-cheeked children, heroic coal miners with rippling muscles working 100 hours a week for the good of the people, and so on. The purpose of art, according to this theory, was to support the Soviet state directly, by showing how wonderful life would be when communism had been fully realized (and not what it is like under the various transitional regimes). Capitalist societies utilize the arts and the culture industries to maintain themselves and to prevent revolution or radical social change.

It is probable that the members of the Frankfurt school, and their followers, were nostalgic for a different period—what might be described as an imaginary golden era—when life was simpler, when members of the cultural elite (as opposed to the economic elite) were given high status and treated with great deference, when values were not in contention, and before the development of the modern bureaucratic capitalistic "mass" society. The Frankfurt school has lost some of its influence in recent years, but many of its ideas are still used, with some modifications and modernizations, by what are known now as "critical" communication theorists, though many critical theorists are not Marxists.

The purpose of the "culture" industry, according to critical theorists, is to manipulate the consciousness of the masses so as to maintain current social and economic and political institutions. This is very useful for those at the top—those who have great wealth and who control the dominant institutions found in capitalist societies—the bourgeoisie, who are the subject of the next section.

The Bourgeoisie

According to Marx, those members of society who own and control the mode of production—the property-owning class—are members of the bourgeoisie. They are opposed by the workers, who own relatively little and who form the proletariat. The bourgeoisie not only owns most of the property in a given society, it also controls the ideas of the proletariat:

> The ideas of the ruling class are, in every age, the ruling ideas: i.e. the class which is the dominant *material* force in society is at the same time its dominant *intellectual* force. The class which has the means of material production at its disposal, has control at the same time over the means of mental production. (Marx, 1964, p. 78)

The bourgeoisie controls the mass media and uses them, as suggested above, to carry hidden ideological messages that support the status quo. In addition, the heroes and heroines in stories controlled by the bourgeoisie tend to be bourgeois characters who spread capitalist ideology (indirectly, in a disguised form) by championing, for example, individualism and the notion of the self-made man or woman, and by helping generate consumer culture and consumer lust. The bourgeoisie is aided, according to Marxist theory, by writers, artists, politicians, managers, and so on—members of the petty bourgeoisie—who help the bourgeoisie maintain its control of the economy and of society. The writers who create texts championing bourgeois values are not doing so consciously, the argument goes. They have been raised in a bourgeois society and have absorbed, unconsciously, bourgeois values, so it is to be expected that their heroes and heroines will reflect such values.

There are also oppositional texts, works that attack capitalism and bourgeois society, but these also are useful to the bourgeoisie, because (a) they have little impact, and (b) they help sustain the illusion that bourgeois societies are free and open to challenge. Bourgeois heroes and heroines are countered in these oppositional texts by Marxist heroes and heroines, whose actions show how people are being exploited and how the masses are given a false consciousness of their state and their possibilities by bourgeois ideology. These Marxist heroic figures expose capitalist ideology and lead revolutions to overthrow the class system and help institute a classless—that is, communist—society, in which each gives according to ability and gets according to need.

In the battle between capitalism and communism, capitalism has clearly been victorious, and most communist societies are trying to institute free market-based economies instead of command economies, though these new societies may not end up identical to (that is, as bourgeois as) U.S. and Western European societies.

The term *bourgeois* is used by some people as a form of personal insult. It suggests that the person so labeled conforms to middle-class patterns of behavior and has middle-class values and tastes. Such a person is perceived to be very self-satisfied and materialistic while lacking refined aesthetic sensibilities (rich, but without style and finesse; perhaps even vulgar and boorish). The stereotypical bourgeois person is seen as relying on expensive stores for guidance in matters of "taste." The notion is that working-class people who somehow become wealthy need to be "socialized" and have to learn proper ways of behaving, dressing, and furnishing their houses if they are to take their place as members of the elite class.

Class

Socioeconomic class is one of the fundamental concepts used by Marxists, as well as by sociologists and other social scientists. Technically speaking, a class is any group with at least one thing in common. As the term is commonly used in cultural criticism, *class* refers to categories based on the economic resources of different groups of people in a given society, and the social and cultural arrangements that stem from this division. That is, economic class divisions have cultural consequences; members of specific classes tend to have similar educational levels, occupations, lifestyles, values, aesthetic sensibilities, and so on, and differ in these respects from members of other socioeconomic classes.

Many social scientists use a ranking system devised by W. Lloyd Warner a number of years ago that divides U.S. society into six socioeconomic classes: upper-upper, lower-upper, upper-middle, lower-middle, upper-lower, and lower-lower. Each of these classes differs considerably from the others in terms of everything from food preferences to the way children are toilet trained, from how houses are furnished to the kinds of education children are given. At the time he wrote, Warner (1953) estimated the proportion of the U.S. population in each socioeconomic class as follows:

upper-upper, 1.4%
lower-upper, 1.6%
upper-middle, 10%
lower-middle, 28%
upper-lower, 33%
lower-lower, 25%

These figures are dated, but the distribution has not changed appreciably. The top 1% of the U.S. population currently controls something like 40% of the wealth (Nason, 1992). Inequity in the distribution of wealth (and thus of political power) is one of the major concerns of Marxist and other critics of U.S. society.

There is in the United States, or perhaps I should say there was, a sense that class is basically irrelevant, and that if a person is willing to work hard enough, he or she can and will succeed. We find this theme in many works of fiction, such as the novels of Horatio Alger, in which heroes with "luck, pluck, and virtue" ultimately succeed. This is part of the concept known as the American Dream, and it has had a powerful influence on U.S. society and U.S. politics. (It has also been ridiculed savagely; Nathanael West's satire *A Cool Million* is one example.) Because success is defined essentially in terms of individual initiative, a psychological or characterological construct, those who do not succeed (and *success* tends to be defined as rising in the class structure) have only themselves to blame. From this viewpoint, institutions that look after the welfare of people are not needed, because opportunity is open to all (in fact, attempts to lift up the poor are considered to be counterproductive). Those who fail, therefore, must lack adequate willpower and determination. But failure, it should be pointed out, is seen as only temporary; the will to succeed must inevitably lead to success, even if there are numerous failures along the way.

In the 1990s, the American Dream seems to have lost some of its power; for the first time in U.S. history, a great proportion of young people are finding that their standard of living is and will continue to be below that of their parents. In addition, many middle-class people find themselves slipping down the class ladder. It also may be that large numbers of recent immigrants, who were not brought up on the American Dream, come from cultures that do not encourage belief in traditional American individualism (a term coined by Alexis de Tocqueville, 1956, to describe a basic American value).

John Fiske and John Hartley (1978) make an interesting distinction between class *in itself* and class *for itself*:

> Class *in itself* involves the *objective existence* of classes produced by a social structure deriving ultimately from what Marx variously terms the material, social or economic "conditions of existence." These classes are differentiated from one another by inequalities of power, wealth, security, opportunity and position. . . . But people's response to their objective class situation gives rise to the secondary notion of class *for itself*. This is the (sometimes only potential) awareness among people of a *common identity* springing from their common experience. (pp. 101-102)

This distinction is important, Fiske and Hartley argue, because television avoids divisions between classes in themselves and tends to focus on classes for themselves, thus downplaying the importance of class.

Alienation

Alienation is, many Marxists suggest, the central concept of Marxism, and one that reflects the humanistic and moral aspects of Marxism, in contrast to erratic and "simplistic" characterizations of this philosophy as based on violence and revolution. We can see that the word *alien* is the root of the term. An alien is a stranger, a person with no ties (liens, lines, connections) with others. Marx believed that capitalism generates alienation in all sections of society, so even the wealthy are not immune to it.

The wealthy, those in the ruling class, who own the means of production, are of necessity alienated from the poor people in society, the proletariat, who are terribly exploited and are the source of the wealth of the ruling classes. But the poor are also victims of alienation; they are alienated from their work, experience themselves only as commodities, and suffer grievously, both physically and psychologically.

In bourgeois societies, workers do not take pleasure in their work, according to Marx; they do it only as a means of satisfying other needs. Workers work not for themselves, but for someone else, and the work belongs to others:

> The *alienation* of the worker in his product means not only that his labour becomes an object, takes on its own existence, but that it exists outside him, independently, and alien to him, and that it stands opposed to him as an autonomous power. The life which he has given to the object sets itself against him as an alien and hostile force. (Marx, 1964, pp. 169-170)

This sense of being a commodity is felt not only by poor manual laborers in contemporary U.S. and other capitalist societies, but also by managerial (petty bourgeois) types who are not in the proletariat per se, but who find themselves exploited and cast aside whenever their superiors (who are also instruments of the ruling class) feel it is necessary. Even professional athletes in the United States, many of whom are multimillionaires, sometimes experience themselves as commodities. They are cast off or traded when their usefulness to their teams is thought to be finished (although in recent years, because of rule changes and various legal decisions, they have found ways of dealing with this matter to some degree).

In socialist societies, so the theory goes, because workers (and everyone else in society) own the means of production, alienation cannot exist. Those who manage the factories supposedly do so in the name and interest of the workers and the people in general. Ironically, it was impossible to get people to work hard in societies that followed Marxist principle (that is, communist societies). The system generated incredible corruption, and the class differences found in communist societies were as great as—or even greater than, in some cases—in capitalist societies. As the saying went about work in communist societies: "We pretend to work and they pretend to pay us."

Some theorists have argued that alienation is too vague a concept; they suggest that evidence of alienation has been found in small villages and in big cities, in ancient civilizations as well as modern societies, and that alienation is not a problem generated by capitalist or Marxist economic and social arrangements but a more or less permanent problem that all people face.

With the collapse of communism in Eastern Europe and the Soviet Union, some Marxist critics now are arguing that these societies were never really Marxist; rather, they were perverted forms of statist socialism. These critics suggest that Marxism remains relevant and has utility as a tool for critique of societies where economic inequality and the things that stem from it—racism, sexism, exploitation, and other such phenomena—generate alienation in people. Marxist critics argue that the alienation Marx found in bourgeois societies had an impact on the psyches of the workers and on everyone else who was taught to lust for commodities as a means of assuaging feelings of hollowness and alienation.

Commodity Fetishism

Marx believed that as a result of the alienation generated by capitalist societies, workers became estranged not only from themselves but also from the products of their labors. This estrangement and commodification is "mysterious" and only partially perceived by the senses. As he writes in *Capital*:

> There is a physical relation between physical things. But it is different with commodities. There, the existence of the things *qua* commodities, and the value-relation between the products of labor which stamps them as commodities, have absolutely no connexion with their physical properties and with the material relations arising therefrom. There it is a definite social relation between men, that assumes, in their eyes, the fantastic form of a relation between things. (Marx, 1972, p. 217)

Social relationships among people are magically transferred to objects. In order to explain this phenomenon, Marx suggests, it is best to find an analogy in religion, a "mist-enveloped" world. He continues:

> In that world the productions of the human brain appear as independent beings endowed with life, and entering into relation both with one another and the human race. So it is in the world of commodities with the products of men's hands. This I call the Fetishism which attaches itself to the products of labour, so soon as they are produced as commodities, and which is therefore inseparable from the production of commodities. (p. 217)

The term *fetish*, as we conventionally use it, has two meanings. It involves a belief that an object has magical powers, and it describes the displacement of sexual desire from a person to an object. Marx uses the term to critique bourgeois societies, and it has also been used, in an updated way, by Marxists such as Wolfgang Haug. Haug (1987) is interested in what he calls "commodity aesthetics," using *aesthetics* in the way it was originally used by scholars, as it applies to the way the senses work and to sensual understanding. For Haug, products are designed "to stimulate in the onlooker the desire to possess and the impulse to buy" (p. 8).

Haug's use of language is worth noting: He uses words such as "stimulate," "desire," "possess," and "impulse," all of which have sexual connotations. Indeed, one of his main arguments is that human sensuality is transformed and remolded in the service of the sale of consumer products. One might say that sexual lust, directed from one person to another, is necessarily displaced onto commodities in bourgeois societies (we move from sexual lust to consumer lust) in order to sell products and keep the economy working at maximum efficiency.

Consumer lust may actually be used in the service of sexual lust—people want to make themselves as attractive as possible to the objects of their affection—but what is crucial is that consumer lust can be activated and controlled. In both cases, aesthetics and human sensuality are utilized. And not only are objects aestheticized, but the act of consumption is turned into an aesthetically satisfying, stylized experience. Haug even suggests that there is currently an attempt to shift the focus from commodities per se to the act of consumption. This is done by conditioning and reshaping the instincts and behavior of the general public and, in particular, of young people, who are most susceptible to this process.

Consumer Culture

According to Marxist cultural critics, capitalist (or bourgeois) societies are able to produce an abundance of material goods, but they also inevitably generate alienation. Thus, though large numbers of people have all kinds of material possessions, they are not happy. People have commodities but also experience themselves as commodities, because their work is alien to their deeper natures and they work to make money so they can survive, not because they feel they are expressing themselves in their work. As Marx (1964) put it: "The *alienation* of the worker in his product means not only that his labour becomes an object, takes on its own existence, but that it exists outside him, independently and alien to him, and that it stands opposed to him as an autonomous power" (pp. 169-170). Our work, Marx adds, is external to us, is not fulfilling, is done only to satisfy other needs, not our personal needs. It is, thus, forced labor.

We work because we have what might be called "real" needs (food, clothing, shelter) and because we are inspired to work to satisfy desires that constantly tempt us, what might be called "unreal needs." This tempting, the creation of this desire, is done by the advertising industry. Marx (1963) discusses this in a famous passage:

> Every man speculates upon creating a *new* need in another in order to force him to a new sacrifice, to place him in a new dependence, and to entice him into a new kind of pleasure and thereby into economic ruin. Everyone tries to establish over others an *alien* power in order to find there the satisfaction of his own egoistic need. (p. 50)

Consumer culture and lust suggest that alienation is functional for those who control the economy, for it is the spiritual anguish and sense of estrangement from the self that leads people to purchase, endlessly, products and services in an effort to alleviate the alienation they feel.

The institution of advertising is of central importance in bourgeois consumer cultures, for it is advertising that makes people aware of the various products to be had and gives products and services symbolic significance. It is advertising that creates fashion (a form of collective behavior), gives people a sense of style, and offers information about what kinds of commodities should be consumed to generate a particular image. There are now many cable television channels devoted to shopping, the most important new genre developed for television since the commercial.

Some theorists of consumer culture, such as Henri Lefebvre (1984), argue that advertising is an extremely powerful force that exerts terror on people and uses terror more or less to force people to behave in certain ways. That is, advertising is more than just a means of marketing products; it is an instrument of social control. Wolfgang Haug (1987) suggests that advertisers have learned to exploit human sexuality, through their use of design in objects and advertising, to keep the consumer culture operating. He argues that advertisers have aestheticized commodities so that these objects themselves now stimulate desire—in addition to the messages we get from advertising agencies. Hans Magnus Enzenberger (1974) argues that advertising's real goal is not to sell goods (the immediate goal), but to sell the political order that makes the consumer culture possible (the long-term goal).

According to Aristotle, people need goods to help them establish a sense of identity. The recent events in Eastern Europe, where people had been deprived of material goods, show that people want to have "the good things in life." The theorists of consumer culture do not attack the notion of people having material goods; rather, they attack the (alleged) overemphasis put on personal consumer goods by individuals in capitalist countries and the frenzy for the acquisition of these goods that is found in consumer cultures. The focus on leisure pursuits and private expenditures breeds privatism, selfishness, and reluctance to take care of social needs and to spend money in the public realm.

Capitalism, from the perspective of consumer culture theorists, is not simply an economic system, but a kind of culture in which almost everything is subordinated to consumption. Our energies, our talents, and our time become devoted to showing that we have taste (and know what to buy, where to eat, where to travel) and power (money to afford these things). There is, then, a culture of capitalism—characterized by an extremely well developed advertising industry, the production of many goods and services in the private realm, and, generally speaking, the increased separation of people into socioeconomic classes, with those at the top of the economic ladder gaining ever-larger amounts of money at the expense of those at the bottom.

Our culture becomes distorted and unbalanced, and we become (without consciously being aware of it) victims of this culture, continually spinning our wheels, so to speak, to show that we can afford the right car, a trophy wife or husband, and so on. Ironically, what is ultimately consumed in bourgeois societies is the consumer, and as the fabric of society deteriorates, owing to privatism and neglect of the public realm, even the lives of the affluent become impoverished.

Advertising is, Marxist critics argue, the central institution responsible for the education of people about products and services that are available in their society and for creating the desire to purchase certain of these products and services. In the United States, where advertising is highly developed, billions of dollars are spent each year on advertising (in all forms, including radio and television commercials, print advertisements, and billboards), and this form of commercial "education" competes with, and in many cases overwhelms, the education available through the society's educational institutions.

Advertising is an industry that uses the services of writers, artists, researchers, actors and actresses, photographers, cinematographers, directors, and many others who are involved in creating and producing print, radio, and television advertisements. Marxist critics argue that advertising has become a crucial industry in capitalist societies. Advertising has also been given the tasks of stimulating productivity in workers (now that the work ethic has declined), so they will have the money they need to buy goods in this consumer culture, and, implicitly, of suggesting that the political order that makes this culture of consumption possible is a good one.

According to Marxist critics, advertising promotes privatism, selfishness, lack of interest in social matters, and attempts to escape from social responsibilities. It gives people illusions about themselves and about the seemingly classless nature of U.S. society. It is also immoral, these critics suggest, because advertisers use whatever techniques they can (moral or immoral) to get people to use their products and services. Thus women are debased and depicted as sexual objects, and people are made to feel anxious about their inability to afford certain products. Whereas the intended function of advertising texts is to sell products or services, it is their unintended functions that give people ideas about how to relate to women, what values are important, and so on—ideas that often go unrecognized and that may be destructive.

Defenders of advertising argue that by generating greater sales, advertising more or less pays for itself; increased sales volume leads to lower unit prices. They also suggest that advertising pays for "free" television in the United States (unlike in some countries, where fees or taxes pay for the production of television programs) and accounts for the relatively low prices of other mass media, such as magazines and newspapers. Supporters also argue that advertising has been responsible, in part, for the creation of a dynamic society, where workers are highly motivated and the standard of living is relatively high.

Critics of advertising tend to focus their attention on its social impact, in general, and on the way that specific print advertisements or radio and television commercials generate meaning and achieve their effects, in particular. In the latter regard, they use critical techniques such as semiotics, psychoanalytic theory, sociological theory, and Marxist theory to analyze relevant texts.

In *The Mechanical Bride*, a pathbreaking analysis of advertising (and comics), Marshall McLuhan (1951) used a number of advertisements to address some interesting aspects of the American psyche and U.S. society in general. He showed the way various print advertisements appealed to fundamental American values, attitudes, and belief systems (some of which we were not aware of). But how do advertisements and other forms of communication work? René Girard's (1991) theory of mimetic desire offers an interesting viewpoint. Because we desire what others desire, advertisements show us people we admire (the beautiful people, celebrities, heroes, gorgeous women, movie stars) and wish to imitate as possessing certain products or using certain services. We purchase these products and services because we believe they are the objects of the desire of those we hold in esteem, and we imitate their desire.

Interpellation

Interpellation is the process by which the representations found in a culture (in media such as television, film, and magazines and in art forms such as advertisements and commercials) coerce, so to speak, individuals into accepting the ideologies carried by these forms of representation. Kaja Silverman (1983) discusses this concept as follows:

The French Marxist philosopher Louis Althusser helps us to understand that discourse may also consist of an exchange between a person and a cultural agent, i.e. a person or a textual construct which relays ideological information. (Althusser isolates priests and educators as particularly important cultural agents, but the description which he offers would apply as well to a television program, a novel, or a film.) The agent addresses the person, and in the process defines not so much its own as the other's identity. In "Ideology and Ideological State Apparatuses," Althusser refers to the address as "hailing" and the successful outcome as "interpellation." Interpellation occurs when the person to whom the agent speaks recognizes him or herself in that speech, and takes up subjective residence there." (pp. 48-49)

What happens is equivalent, Althusser explains, to hailing a person, using language such as "Hey, you!" The person hailed stops and turns around, recognizing that he or she is the person addressed. In this "hailing" process, which is analogous to shouting at people, ideological belief systems, by dominating the systems of representation found in a society, either recruit people directly or transform individuals into subjects who learn to identify with the representation (and its ideology) doing the hailing.

The theory of interpellation suggests that we accept ideologies by identifying with characters and situations found in the arts and mass media, and inserting ourselves, much as Woody Allen did in *Zelig*, into the scheme of things. Regardless of whatever else they do, the arts, the media, and our collective representations in general end up having an ideological function.

Ideology

An ideology is a systematic and comprehensive set of ideas relating to and explaining social and political life. Ideologies "explain" to people why things happen and, in so doing, tend to justify the status quo. As Alexander Pope put it so succinctly, "Whatever is, is right." Claus Mueller (1973) defines *ideology* as follows:

> Ideologies are . . . integrated belief systems which provide expla-
> nations for political reality and establish the collective goals of a class
> or group, and in the case of a dominant ideology, of society at large.
> They have an evaluative component in that they attach either nega-
> tive or positive judgments to conditions in society and to political
> goals. (pp. 101-102)

One of the more important aspects of ideologies is that they are
often not recognized, or fully understood, by those who hold them,
and their implications are not seen. Karl Mannheim (1936) has
dealt with this aspect of ideological thought:

> The concept "ideology" reflects the one discovery which emerged
> from political conflict, namely, that ruling groups can in their thinking
> become so intensively interest-bound to a situation that they are
> simply no longer able to see certain facts which would undermine
> their sense of domination. There is implicit in the word "ideology"
> the insight that in certain situations the collective unconscious of
> certain groups obscures the real condition of society both to itself
> and to others and thereby stabilizes it. (p. 40)

There is, then, a functional aspect to ideology: It serves the interest
of ruling groups and stabilizes society, and it deludes those groups
that do not rule about their situation, their possibilities, their real
interests.

Mannheim contrasts ideologists with utopians, those from
oppressed groups who see only the negative aspects of a given
society and whose only interest is in radically transforming or
destroying that society. Like the ideologists, the utopians do not
see society in realistic terms. The ideologists want to maintain the
status quo, and the utopians think only of major changes they
would like to make in society.

Marxist critics of media and culture have a great interest in the
ideological aspects of cultural practices and texts, and try to point
out the ideological messages hidden in these practices and texts.
As Donald Lazere (1977) notes:

> Applied to any aspect of culture, Marxist method seeks to explicate
> the manifest and latent or coded reflections of modes of material

production, ideological values, class relations and structures of social power—racial or sexual as well as politico-economic—or the state of consciousness of people in a precise historical or socio-economic situation. . . . The Marxist method, recently in varying degrees of combination with structuralism and semiology, has provided an incisive analytic tool for studying the political signification in every facet of contemporary culture, including popular entertainment in TV and films, music, mass circulation books, newspaper and magazine features, comics, fashion, tourism, sports and games, as well as such acculturating institutions as education, religion, the family and child-rearing, social and sexual relations between men and women—all the patterns of work, play, and other customs of everyday life. . . . The most frequent theme in Marxist cultural criticism is the way the prevalent mode of production and ideology of the ruling class in any society dominate every phase of culture, and at present, the way capitalist production and ideology dominate American culture, along with that of the rest of the world that American business and culture have colonized. (pp. 755-756)

This ideology produces, Marxists claim, false consciousness in the general public—a sense that things are the way they have to be, that success is a function of willpower (the American Dream), and that matters of socioeconomic class in the United States, an egalitarian nation, are relatively unimportant.

Marxists, who search single-mindedly and with great passion for the ideological (or allegedly ideological) content of mass media and culture, are what Mannheim calls utopians, in that their focus is only on the way the ruling class perpetuates its power through spreading ideological messages. Marxist critics tend to neglect aesthetic and other aspects of texts. The zeal of the communists in the Soviet Union and elsewhere was, it seems, of the same nature as that of the inquisitors in the Middle Ages; both were willing to sacrifice people, in large numbers, for utopian considerations (a classless society for the communists, a society devoid of unbelievers for the inquisitors).

Mannheim (1936) offers an important insight into ideological belief, and belief in general, and that is that belief is tied to group membership:

From a purely functionalist point of view, the derivation of our meanings, whether they be true or false, plays an indispensable role,
namely, it socializes events for a group. We belong to a group not
only because we are born into it, not merely because we profess to
belong to it, nor finally because we give it our loyalty and alle-
giance, but primarily because we see the world and certain things
in the world the way it does (i.e. in terms of the meanings of the
group in question). In every concept, in every concrete meaning, there
is contained a crystallization of the experiences of a certain group.
(pp. 21-22)

Our interest in ideology is connected, then, to our identification with a group of thinkers and theorists who believe that ideological considerations are of great importance, and that revealing
the ideological aspects of cultural practices and the ideological
messages found in mass-mediated texts is a means of changing
the political order. This matter is to be dealt with not only in particular countries; it also has implications that go beyond the
borders of the United States and other countries of the First World,
as we shall see in the discussion that follows.

Cultural Imperialism

Cultural imperialism is a term used by a number of Marxist thinkers (and others, such as critical thinkers) to describe the effects of
the distribution of Western mass media (U.S. media in particular)
throughout the world. Critics argue that the mass media of the
United States spread bourgeois values and thus indoctrinated
people, particularly those in the Third World, with capitalist ideology. This, in turn, makes it easier for these people to be exploited
and prevents the development of class solidarity and consciousness concerning what is really going on in their societies. The
cultural imperialism hypothesis, sometimes known as the theory
of "Coca-Colonization," is quite controversial.

According to this hypothesis, the creators of works of popular
art are not consciously working to spread American values and
beliefs. These bourgeois values and beliefs are held by most

people in the United States, and it is only natural for them to be found in our comics, movies, television shows, and other forms of popular culture. Two Chilean Marxists, Ariel Dorfman and Armand Mattelart, have written a book titled *How to Read Donald Duck: Imperialist Ideology in the Disney Comic* (1991), in which they argue that Disney comics are, ultimately, instruments of U.S. ideological and cultural domination.

A second idea, connected with this, is that U.S. culture (and other powerful cultures, such as those found in Western Europe) is overwhelming fragile Third World cultures and spreading American and Western European beliefs, values, and, in some cases, popular culture: fast-food restaurants, Levi's, rock and roll, and so on. Americans are the worst offenders because we sell the most films and television shows to Third World and other countries, who cannot afford to produce their own films and television shows. We are, then, surreptitiously spreading our ideological beliefs and, at the same time, destroying allegedly fragile cultures, which will eventually lead to a kind of blandness and a homogenized universal shopping mall-like plasticity to life everywhere on the planet.

The cultural imperialism hypothesis is based on the notion that the mass media are very powerful and have an enormous impact on people, and that those people in the Third World who decode the works spread by the media do so in ways relatively similar to Americans. But semioticians have argued that people decode texts in widely different ways, depending on their cultural backgrounds, socioeconomic levels, and so on, and reader-response theorists argue that each individual makes sense of a text in his or her own way. Furthermore, some communication theorists argue that the mass media are not as powerful as we tend to think they are. Thus there are reasons to doubt the validity of the cultural imperialism hypothesis and its proponents' dire predictions.

There is another argument that Marxist theorists make that would explain why people might be dominated and not recognize it. They suggest that people are dominated and controlled at a higher level of abstraction than the ideological; it is to this theory that we now turn.

Hegemony

The term *hegemony* was coined by Antonio Gramsci, an Italian Marxist. The traditional definition of the term involves the concept of political domination, control, and rule, especially in reference to sovereign states. Gramsci used the term in a different manner, suggesting that hegemony has psychocultural implications. What Gramsci wanted to do was show how the dominant classes were able to convince those who were being exploited that their situation was natural and thus universal, which meant that things could not be changed. According to this thinking, it is the cultural institutions (which are in the realm of the superstructure) that are dominant or play a major role in convincing people to accept the status quo, not the base and economic relations. Raymond Williams (1977) interprets hegemony as follows:

> "Hegemony" is a concept which at once includes and goes beyond two powerful earlier concepts: that of "culture" as a "whole social process," in which men define and shape their whole lives; and that of "ideology," in any of its Marxist senses, in which a system of meanings and values is the expression or projection of a particular class interest.
>
> "Hegemony" goes beyond "culture," as previously defined, in its insistence on relating the "whole social process" to specific distributions of power and influence. . . . It is in just the recognition of the *wholeness* of the process that the concept of "hegemony" goes beyond "ideology." What is decisive is not only the conscious system of ideas and beliefs, but the whole lived process as practically organized by specific and dominant meanings and values. Ideology, in its normal senses, is a relatively formal and articulated system of meanings, values, and beliefs, of a kind that can be abstracted as a "world view" or a "class outlook." (pp. 108-109)

There is a difference, then, between ideology and hegemony. Hegemony is more pervasive, more abstract, and dominates everyday life, our assumptions, the world of what "goes without saying." Williams uses the term *saturate* to describe how hegemonic thought fills our lives. We are conscious, or can be made conscious, of ideologies, and that is one of the main purposes of Marxist cultural criticism; hegemony—or, more precisely, hegemonic domination—is a process that we find hard to discover because it is so ubiquitous and amorphous.

One way of understanding this concept is to say that whereas ideological domination involves the political realm, hegemonic domination involves the social and cultural realms, areas where it is much more difficult to isolate and understand, because it is, Williams (1977) suggests, "our lived system of meanings and values" (p. 110). Hegemonic domination is thus more widespread, more hidden or disguised, and more complete than ideological domination, which has "parameters" that can be located and addressed. Marxist critics often combine the two terms and talk about "ideological hegemonic domination," covering all the bases.

Williams suggests that much of the opposition to the dominant culture is still hegemonic and thus only illusory; it still takes place within the framework of what is allowed by the dominant culture. But not all opposition is illusory, and this leads to one of the most important theoretical problems of cultural analysis: Which analyses are truly oppositional and outside of hegemonic domination and which are only seemingly oppositional and dominated by hegemonic imperatives? The solution Williams suggests is that we maintain openness in our analyses, which is reasonable given that works of art, as signifying systems, are also open and subject to many different analyses.

There is a philosophical problem connected to the concept of hegemony: If it is all-pervasive, how did we discover it in the first place? If all knowledge is social, how do we discover this? The answer, it has been suggested, is that some people are "improperly" socialized and thus are able to see things that most people, who have been "properly" socialized, are blind to. Whether this answer will satisfy everyone is another matter.

In a similar vein, we are all exposed to so much media, to so many "reproductions" of works, that it is hard to distinguish between what is "original" and what is "reproduced," or to gain an understanding of what "reproductions" are and what effects they might be having upon us. That is our next topic.

Reproduction

The mass media are based, in large measure, upon our ability to "reproduce" phenomena: to make photographs; to print newspapers, magazines, and books; to capture performances on film and videotape; to record sounds on various media. Walter Benjamin, a German Marxist critic, in an important essay titled "The Work of Art in the Age of Mechanical Reproduction" (1974), raises a number of points about our ability to reproduce original works of art mechanically (and now we would add photoelectronically). He suggests that original works of art are unique; they have an "aura" and possess an "authority" and authenticity that is lost when they are reproduced. Original works often are connected to rituals; they have what might be described as sacred dimensions, so that people maintain a kind of distance from them.

In an age of reproduction, however, people are not interested in being kept distant from things and accept the mechanical reproduction of an object as its equivalent, and as a consumer good rather than a hallowed work. In addition, people respond to works not on an individual basis, but collectively, generally as part of an unrecognized massification or mobilization of acceptance.

> For the first time in world history, mechanical reproduction emancipates the work of art from its parasitical dependence on ritual. To an ever greater degree, the work of art reproduced becomes the work of art designed for reproducibility. From a photographic negative, for example, one can make any number of prints; to ask for the "authentic" print makes no sense. But the instant criterion of authenticity ceases to be applicable to artistic production, the total function of art is reversed. Instead of being based on ritual, it begins to be based on another practice, politics. (Benjamin, 1974, pp. 618-619)

Thus the development of various means of reproduction has meant a major shift in the function of the arts, which become tied up with economic considerations and political matters. In general, the artist no longer works from an inner vision; rather, he or she is guided by social acceptance and the tastes of a potential mass audience. Films, from this perspective, are not merely entertainments; they become tied to political mass movements and are used as instruments of ideological battle.

In the epilogue to his article, Benjamin suggests that both fascism and communism attempt to use art for their own purposes. Fascism, he suggests, tries to organize the masses by keeping property rights but allowing people to express themselves. This leads to "the introduction of aesthetics into political life" (Benjamin, 1974, p. 633) and ultimately to war, which becomes aestheticized as well:

> Mankind, which in Homer's time was an object of contemplation for the Olympian gods, now is one for itself. Its self-alienation has reached such a degree that it can experience its own self-destruction as an aesthetic pleasure of the first order. This is the situation of politics which Fascism is rendering aesthetic. Communism responds by politicizing art. (p. 634)

Benjamin extends this notion of aestheticization to everyday life in his book on the department stores and arcades of Paris, which he believed created dream worlds and generated fantasies in the minds of people frequenting such places.

Wolfgang Haug, as we have seen, picked up on Benjamin's theory of aestheticization and developed it, adding an economic component and tying it to commodities—the objects and artifacts that play so large a part in our lives. It is useful to move from this focus on the difference between original works and reproductions and on the impact that all the reproductions found in the mass media might be having upon us to a broader perspective on politics, an innovative and very fruitful way of looking at the political cultures that exist in democratic societies.

Political Cultures

At one time political scientists were extremely enthusiastic about the role that studies of political culture might play in their discipline. Then, for some reason (perhaps because it did not lend itself to that quantification so dear to the hearts of contemporary social scientists), they lost interest in it. Now, however, it is staging a comeback.

Political culture refers to the impact of politics on culture and the impact of culture on politics. More specifically, political culture involves the values, beliefs, ideas, and practices found in groups that play a role in the political ordering of societies. As Lucian Pye (1962) notes, "Political culture is shaped on the one hand by the general historical experience of the society or system and on the other hand by the intensely private and personal experiences of individuals as they become members of first the society and then the polity" (p. 121). Pye (1962, pp. 122-124) then lists a number of considerations to be kept in mind in the analysis of political cultures:

1. the scope of activities, issues, and decisions perceived by people as relevant to the management of political power
2. the body of wisdom and knowledge of the people that makes it possible for them to comprehend and find meaning in, explain, and predict the behaviors they perceive as being relevantly political
3. the faith beyond substantive knowledge that is governed by the prophetic words of those perceived as appropriate spokesmen of the future
4. the values assumed to be most sensitive to political actions
5. the standards accepted as valid for appraising and evaluating political conduct
6. the legitimate identities people can assume in contending for power and the common identity that the polity provides for all

What we are dealing with, ultimately, are the values that people have internalized and made part of their belief systems and everyday lives. We study political culture because we assume that it will help us understand the way people make the choices they do in the political world and how different political systems function. The focus is an indirect one—not on political institutions and the way they function, but on the values and beliefs people have that lead them to create specific political organizations and political orders. The concept of culture is important because it suggests that people's values and beliefs are tied to groups they belong to, and do not just pop into their heads from out of the blue (as noted above, in the discussion of Mannheim's work).

Aaron Wildavsky (1989) suggests that in democratic societies one finds four political cultures:

> The dimensions of cultural theory are based on answers to two questions: Who am I? and What shall I do? The question of identity may be answered by saying that individuals belong to a strong group, a collective that makes decisions binding on all members or that their ties are weak in that their choices bind only themselves. The question of action is answered by responding that the individual is subject to many or few prescriptions, a free spirit or a spirit tightly constrained. The strength or weakness of group boundaries and the numerous or few, varied or similar prescriptions binding or freeing individuals are the components of their culture.

When we consider together the strength of group boundaries and the number and variety of prescriptions on individuals, we get four groups, which Wildavsky labels elitists, individualists, egalitarians, and fatalists. (In recent work, Wildavsky has suggested a fifth group, which is very small; I will not consider that group here, because it is not significant to the discussion at hand.) Elitists believe in hierarchy and have a sense of responsibility to those beneath them. Individualists believe essentially in free competition and that the government should maintain a level playing field and protect property. Egalitarians stress that everyone has common needs, criticize the elitists and the individualists, and try to raise the fatalists. (Marxists, of course, are strong egalitarians.) Fatalists believe in luck and are essentially apolitical. Individuals are not locked into political cultures for life; they can move from one group to another, depending on their experiences.

Wildavsky (1989) focuses our attention on the cultural dimensions of politics and the role that membership in groups (that is, the four political cultures) plays in politics. Knowing which group one belongs to and which groups one does not belong to enables people with relatively little information to develop preferences and to make many different political decisions. Political cultures also affect what people read and what they watch on television, because it is logical for individuals to seek out texts that support or reinforce their values and beliefs and to avoid texts that challenge those values and beliefs (and that would lead to dissonance).

"Culture," Wildavsky (1989) states, "is the India rubber man of politics, for it permits preferences to be formed from the slimmest clue" (p. 40). Knowing how cultures are formed and how they influence political behavior becomes, then, a major area for research, because the impact of a kind of political culture is not automatic, and people are often involved in the process of moving from one political culture to another.

Conclusion

With the demise of communist governments in the Soviet Union and Eastern Europe and the general discrediting of communism, the utility of Marxist theories for analyzing culture must be considered. Despite the revelations about the corruption of the governments that ruled in Marx's name and the eagerness with which the countries in what used to be the Soviet Union are embracing market-based economic systems, Marxist critics still claim that they have a role to play. They point out the degree of inequality in many societies, and they provide insights that enable us to understand the arts and media and the role they and other cultural phenomena play in contemporary societies. These topics are the focus of much cultural criticism. Many Marxist critics never believed in communism or were positive about the various communist regimes in Eastern Europe, the Soviet Union, China, and Cuba. These critics use Marxism as a perspective from which to attack what they see as the negative, corrupting, inhumane aspects of Western bourgeois societies, and argue that Marxist views about culture still have validity and utility.

In Wildavsky's typology, it is the egalitarians who are either Marxists or are most like the Marxists (both stress the equality of human needs) and who function as critics of both the elitists and the individualists and champions of the fatalists and those elements in society that suffer from inequalities of one sort or another.

Marxism may have been a failure on the economic and political front, but it still appeals to many cultural critics and other scholars, who use its concepts (often in modified and updated forms) to attack the inequities found in capitalist and, in some cases, socialist societies. Marxism is, some theorists claim, a humanistic philosophy, but its realization in communism led—as utopian visions often do—to immense cruelty and great suffering.

But capitalism, too, has led to cruelty and suffering. Capitalism has been, and some would say still is, characterized by the exploitation of millions of people, by societies in which class differences grow larger and larger, and, as a vast substratum of people who are terribly poor and increasingly desperate grows, by random violence and a great deal of criminal behavior. The old joke about communism and capitalism sums things up nicely: Capitalism is a system in which man exploits his fellow man; under communism, the opposite takes place.

Roland Barthes

4

Semiotics and Cultural Criticism

In this chapter I address some of the basic concepts in semiotics, to show how it enables us to find meaning in texts and other phenomena. I try to explain each concept as simply as possible, and I quote extensively from important passages written by various authorities, to give the reader some idea of how these writers express themselves. There is, however, a certain amount of technical language involved with semiotic analysis that cannot be avoided. There are many advanced books on semiotics available for those who wish to pursue the study of semiotic theory and applied semiotic analysis; interested readers will find several such titles in the list of suggested further reading that follows the final chapter in this volume.

Semiotics can be seen as a form of applied linguistics; semiotic analysis has been applied to everything from fashion to advertising, from James Bond stories to *Star Wars*. The most fundamental concept in semiotics is the sign; semiotic theorists posit human beings as sign-making and sign-interpreting animals. It is with signs that this discussion of semiotics and cultural criticism begins.

Signs in Semiotics and Semiology

Semiotics is, literally speaking, the science of signs. The word *semiotics* comes from the Greek root *semeion*, or sign, and is used to describe a systematic attempt to understand what signs are and how they function. Semiotics is probably the more commonly used term, but some students of signs use the term *semiology*— literally "words" (*logos*) "about signs" (*semeion*). Semiotics is associated with the work of the American philosopher C. S. Peirce (although its roots are in medieval philosophy) and semiology with the work of the Swiss linguist Ferdinand de Saussure. Both are concerned with how meaning is generated and communicated. In his posthumously published book *A Course in General Linguistics*, Saussure (1966) states:

> Language is a system of signs that express ideas, and is therefore comparable to a system of writing, the alphabet of deaf-mutes, military signals, etc. But it is the most important of all these systems.
>   *A science that studies the life of signs within society* is conceivable; it would be part of social psychology and consequently of general psychology; I shall call it *semiology* (from Greek, semeion "sign"). Semiology would show what constitutes signs, what laws govern them. (p. 16)

This may be looked upon as one of the charter statements about semiotics/semiology.

Saussure suggests that signs are made of two parts: a signifier (sound, object, image, or the like) and a signified (concept). The relation that exists between the signifier and the signified is arbitrary, based on convention, or, to use the technical term, *unmotivated*. Because of this fact, we develop and use codes to help us learn what some signs mean.

In addition, Saussure asserts that concepts do not mean anything in themselves; they gain their meanings only relationally, or differentially: "Concepts are purely differential and defined not by their positive characteristics but negatively by their relations with the other terms of the system" (p. 117). For all practical purposes, the most important relationship among terms is binary opposition.

One difference between semiotics and semiology is that semiotics draws its basic ideas from a trichotomy elaborated by C. S.

Peirce (1931-1935, 1958). According to Peirce, there are three kinds of signs—icons, indexes, and symbols:

> Every sign is determined by its object, either first, by partaking in the characters of the object, when I call a sign an *Icon*; secondly, by being really and in its individual existence connected with the individual object, when I call the sign an *Index*; thirdly, by more or less approximate certainty that it will be interpreted as denoting the object, in consequence of a habit (which term I use as including a natural disposition), when I call the sign a *Symbol*. (quoted in Zeyman, 1977, p. 36)

Because semiotics is concerned with everything that can be seen as a sign, and given that just about everything can be seen as a sign (that is, substituting for something else), semiotics emerges as a kind of master science that has utility in all areas of knowledge, especially in the humanities, arts, and social sciences. It has been used, as noted above, in criticism of the fine arts, literature, film, and popular fiction as well as in interpreting architecture, in studying fashion, in analyzing facial expression, in interpreting magazine advertisements and radio and television commercials, in medicine, and in many other areas. Let us consider signs now in a bit more detail, with a focus on how they function.

How Signs Function

A sign can also be defined as anything that can be used to stand for something else, but understanding how signs function is somewhat complicated, because, for Peirce and semioticians, there are always "others" involved. According to Peirce, a sign "is something which stands to somebody for something in some respect or capacity" (1977, p. 27). He adds a philosophical point:

> It seems a strange thing, when one comes to ponder over it, that a sign should leave its interpreter to supply part of its meaning; but the explanation of the phenomenon lies in the fact that the entire universe—not merely the universe of existents, but all that wider

universe, embracing the universe of existents as a part, the universe which we are all accustomed to refer to as "the truth"—that all this universe is perfused with signs, if it is not composed exclusively of signs. (Peirce; epigraph in Sebeok, 1977, p. vi)

If the universe is perfused with, if not composed exclusively of, signs, then humans are, of necessity, semiotic animals—whatever else they may be (rational creatures, tool makers, featherless bipeds, and so on).

Umberto Eco (1976) has added an insight worth considering. If signs can be used to tell the truth, they can also be used to lie:

> Semiotics is concerned with everything that can be taken as a sign. A sign is everything which can be taken as significantly substituting for something else. This something else does not necessarily have to exist or to actually be somewhere at the moment in which a sign stands for it. Thus semiotics is in principle the discipline studying everything which can be used in order to lie. If something cannot be used to tell a lie, conversely it cannot be used to tell the truth; it cannot be used "to tell" at all. (p. 7)

Phenomena such as wigs, dyed hair, elevator shoes, imitation foods, impersonators, and impostors all involve "lying" with signs.

Saussure (1966) first describes signs as being made of a concept and a sound-image: "The linguistic sign unites, not a thing and a name, but a concept and a sound-image" (p. 66). He later modifies his definition:

> I propose to retain the word *sign* [*signe*] to designate the whole and to replace *concept* and *sound-image* respectively by *signified* [*singifie*] and *signifier* [*signifiant*]; the last two terms have the advantage of indicating the opposition that separates them from the whole of which they are parts. (p. 67)

He uses the term *semiology* to describe the science that would study "the life of signs within society," originally placing semiology within social psychology. He suggests that a sign is like a piece of paper: One side is the signifier and the other is the signified, and together they make the sign/sheet of paper. Symbols, however, are a different matter.

Symbols in Saussure's System

A symbol is a subcategory of a sign. It is a sign whose meaning is not completely arbitrary or conventional. Saussure (1966) explains:

> The word *symbol* has been used to designate the linguistic sign, or more specifically, what is here called the signifier. . . . One characteristic of the symbol is that it is never wholly arbitrary; it is not empty, for there is the rudiment of a natural bond between the signifier and the signified. The symbol of justice, a pair of scales, could not be replaced by just any other symbol, such as a chariot. (p. 68)

Peirce sees the symbol as conventional, unlike the icon and index, which are not conventional in his view of things.

What is important about symbols is that they stand for something, they convey meanings. These meanings are often connected to historical events, traditions, and so on. The symbol, generally an object or an image, because it can represent historical events, because it "contains" all kinds of extraneous matters connected to it, because it can be a repository of meanings, because it can have so many connotations, can become very important to people. Think of religious icons, for example. Carl Jung (1968) explains this matter in some detail in his book *Man and His Symbols*:

> Thus a word or an image is symbolic when it implies something more than its obvious and immediate meaning. It has a wider "unconscious" aspect that is never precisely defined or fully explained. Nor can one hope to define or explain it. As the mind explores the symbol, it is led to ideas that lie beyond the grasp of reason. (p. 4)

We are profoundly affected by symbolic phenomena, Jung suggests, all the time—when we are awake and when we dream.

As Freud has pointed out, in our dreams we use the processes of symbolic condensation and displacement to disguise our real thoughts and desires and evade the dream censor. It would wake us up if it recognized the sexual content of our dreams, as manifested, for example, in phallic symbols and symbols of the female genitals. In our visual and literary arts we also use symbolization in an attempt to generate certain responses—assuming there is common understanding of what specific symbols mean (which is not always the case, of course).

In literary criticism, for example, we often find that the study of symbolism in texts is connected with an investigation of their mythic elements—what might be called a myth and symbol school of analysis. Heroes and heroines in novels and plays and films often have symbolic dimensions: What they say and what they do often are symbolic and allegorical as well as connected, indirectly, to the actions of ancient mythic heroes and heroines. That is why some critics argue that all texts are intertextually related to other texts, even though audiences may not be aware of the fact or the creators of texts aware of what they have done.

It is because texts of all kinds—films, television programs, novels, plays, works of visual art—are full of symbolic phenomena (objects, actions of characters, geographic locations, and so on) that they resist easy interpretation. Their symbolic (and mythic) aspects make them extremely complex, and so they are seldom easily understood.

Icon, Index, Symbol: Peirce's System

In Peirce's theory of semiotics there are three kinds of signs: icons, which communicate by resemblance; indexes, which communicate by logical connection; and symbols, which are purely conventional and whose meanings have to be learned. Peirce developed an extremely involved theory of signs, but it rests on the cornerstone of his trichotomy—icon, index, and symbol. He differs from Saussure, who argues that the relationship between a signifier (sound, object) and its signified (concept) is arbitrary

TABLE 4.1 Peirce's Trichotomy

Kind of Sign	*Icon*	*Index*	*Symbol*
Example	pictures	smoke/fire	words, flags
Signify by	resemblance	causal connection	convention
Process	can see	can figure out	must learn

and based on convention (except in the case of the symbol, where the relationship is quasi-motivated or quasi-natural).

In Peirce's theory, both icons and indexes have natural relationships with what they stand for: for example, a portrait of someone and the person being portrayed (an icon) and smoke indicating fire (an index). The meanings of symbols, on the other hand, have to be learned. Table 4.1 presents Peirce's trichotomy in graphic form. Semiotics is important, Peirce argues, because the universe is in essence a system of signs. Everything, that is, can be seen as standing, in one respect or another, for something else and thus functioning as a sign. Let us now look at one aspect of Peirce's trichotomy in a little more detail.

Images

An image is conventionally understood to be a visible representation of something, though it can also be a mental picture of something (such as the image of the businessman as found in early-20th-century American literature). We live in a world of photoelectronic images, and with the development of television, all kinds of images that we never would have seen in real life are now brought to us, in mediated form, on the video tube. As the result of developments in printing, photography, and video, images play an increasingly important role in our lives. Indeed, some scholars suggest that we have moved from a *logocentric* (word-centered) to an *occulocentric* (image-centered) world, with sight exercising hegemony or domination over our other senses.

From a semiotic perspective, a visual image is a collection of what Peirce would call signs, which means that, for example, in

TABLE 4.2 Symbols and Meanings in a 15th-Century Painting

Symbol	Meaning
lighted candle in chandelier	presence of Christ, ardor of the couple
convex mirror	eye of God
dog	marital faithfulness
bride's hand on her stomach	willingness to bear children
fruit on table	Virgin Mary

a print advertisement we have icons, indexical phenomena, and symbols. Icons are relatively easy to interpret because they communicate by resemblance, but understanding indexical signs involves finding some kind of a relationship between signs and their meanings, and symbols are purely conventional, which means we must learn their meanings. In considering images with which we are not familiar, such as paintings from earlier periods, we may not recognize the symbology, so our understanding of the messages conveyed in such images may be relatively primitive.

Let me offer an example. In the painting by Jan Van Eyck titled *Giovanni Arnolfini and His Bride,* painted in 1434, we find a number of symbols whose meanings are not evident to most people in the late 20th century. The painting shows a man holding hands with his wife (who looks pregnant and has her hand on her stomach) in an ornate room. Behind the two figures we see a convex mirror, lighted candles in a chandelier, and a small table with fruit on it. In front of the couple we see a dog. Table 4.2 lists the symbolic objects or representations in the painting and their meanings for people of the period. Today, most would not know the meanings of many of these symbols (or even recognize that candles and dogs could have symbolic meaning), but the symbology would have been evident to many people living in 1434. Just as we may not recognize the significance of symbolic phenomena from earlier times, we may be blind to the symbolic significance of phenomena from different cultures.

When we look at an image (a painting, an advertisement, a work of sculpture, an object) we can look at it in two opposing ways, according to art historian Alois Riegl. Claude Gandelman (1991) discusses Riegl's theories:

> Riegl stated that one type of artistic procedure, which corresponds to a certain way of looking, is based on the scanning of objects according to their outlines. This trajectory Riegl called the optical. The opposite type of vision, which focuses on surfaces and emphasizes the value of the superficies of objects, Riegl called the haptical (from the Greek *haptein*, "to seize, grasp" or *haptikos*, "capable of touching").
>
> On the level of artistic creation, the optical look—if the eye belongs to the painter—produces linearity and angularity, whereas haptic creativity focuses on surfaces. Using Riegl's formula, all forms of art may be grouped under the heading "Outline and/or color in plane and volume." . . . The optical eye merely brushes the surface of things. The haptic, or tactile, eye penetrates in depth, finding its pleasure in textile and grain. (p. 5)

From the haptic perspective, vision becomes a form of touching. Riegl was not the first person to deal with this notion (it is found in the work of Descartes and Berkeley, also, Gandelman points out), but his calling our attention to these two opposing ways of perception is important. It is also possible, of course, to combine these two perspectives.

If seeing haptically is a form of touching, it would suggest that our relation to images is much more complicated than we might suppose. We do not simply glance at images and put them out of our minds; our experience of looking is much more powerful than that. This might explain, in part, the phenomenon of *scopophilia*, literally "looking (*scopo*) loving (*philia*)," a psychological phenomenon involving people who derive sexual pleasure from looking at others or, in the case of *autoscopophilia*, from looking at themselves.

Images, then, play a significant role in our lives, whether we recognize this to be the case or not. They have to be interpreted, and this takes a good deal of work, for it is not always easy to understand how images function.

Cultural critics have, in recent years, expanded upon their interest in images and now talk about the phenomenon of representation. This concept (addressed previously, in Chapter 3) deals with images of all kinds in the context of the social and political order in which these images are found, and considers such matters as who creates images, who controls the image making in a society (especially images generated and spread by the mass media), and the functions these images have for the sociopolitical order and for individuals.

Codes

At the simplest level, codes are systems for interpreting the meanings of various kinds of communication in which the meanings are not obvious or evident. Consider the two apparently meaningless "words" below:

D	P	E	F	T
B	N	C	D	R

As soon as I tell you that the codes for interpreting these series of letters are, respectively, plus 1 and minus 1, you can easily find that both are coded ways of saying *codes*:

D	P	E	F	T	
C	O	D	E	S	(plus one)
B	N	C	D	R	(minus one)

In the world of espionage, messages are often coded (so that if they are somehow intercepted they will not be understood). The same applies to the world of culture. Much of what we see and hear around us in our culture carries messages, but because we do not know the codes that enable us to find the meanings in these messages, we do not pay any attention to them, or, if we do, we tend to interpret them incorrectly. We also tend to be blind to the codes that we have learned because they seem natural to us; we do not realize that when we find meaning in things, we are actually decoding signs. We are like Molière's character who had not realized he was speaking prose all the time.

There are in every society, semioticians suggest, culture codes—hidden structures (in the sense that we are not aware of them or pay no attention to them) that shape our behavior. These codes deal with aesthetic judgments, moral beliefs, cuisine, and many other things. They are directive and generally are highly articulated and specific, even though those who use them tend to be unaware of them. We need codes because we need consistency in our lives. Codes vary in scope from the universal to the local.

If the relationship between a word and the object it stands for, or a signifier and a signified, is arbitrary and based on convention, as Saussure suggests, and symbols are purely conventional, as Peirce suggests, then we need codes to tell us how to know what words mean and what signifiers and symbols mean. The meaning is arbitrary, based on convention, not natural. Thus, by extension, what we call culture can be looked upon as a collection or system of codes, analogous in many respects to language.

Terence Hawkes (1977) addresses this relationship; in discussing the work of the French cultural anthropologist Claude Lévi-Strauss, he writes:

> He attempts to perceive the constituents of cultural behavior, ceremonies, rites, kinship relations, marriage laws, methods of cooking, totemic systems, not as intrinsic or discrete entities, but in terms of the contrastive relationships they have with each other that makes their structures analogous to the phonemic structure of language. (p. 34)

Thus the work of cultural critics involves the process of decoding texts of various kinds in many different realms: words, images, objects, literary and subliterary works, social rituals, food preparation, socialization of children, and numerous other areas.

Creators of texts that are distributed through mass media have a problem of difference between their own codes and the codes of the audiences for these texts, who may (and probably often do) decode them differently from the way the creators intended. In such cases, it is difficult to avoid what Umberto Eco calls "aberrant decoding." This problem exists in other areas as well—for instance, when individuals who have been socialized (that is, have learned codes for behavior) in subcultures become members of

mainstream institutions and have difficulty in behaving "properly" (e.g., when a member of a motorcycle gang becomes a student
at a university).

We now move on to discussion of two concepts that affect cultural meaning in rather specific ways: connotation and denotation.

Connotation

Connotation is a term used to describe the cultural meanings
attached to a term—and, by extension, an image, a figure in a text,
or even a text. In contrast, *denotation* refers to the literal meaning
of a term, figure, text, or so on. *Connotation* comes from the Latin
connotare, "to mark along with." Thus connotation deals with the
historic, symbolic, and emotional matters suggested by or that
"go along with" a term.

Take the figure of James Bond as an example. From a denota-
tive point of view, he is the hero of a number of popular spy novels
and films. But the connotations of James Bond extend to such
matters as sexism, racism, absurd images of the British held by
others, Bond's personal idiosyncrasies, the nature of the British
intelligence establishment, the Cold War, images of Americans
and Russians, and so on.

In his *Mythologies* (1972), Roland Barthes deals with the mythic
significance or what could be called the cultural connotations of
a number of phenomena of everyday life in France, such as wrestling, steak and chips, toys, Garbo's face, and the striptease. His
purpose is to take the world of "what-goes-without-saying" and
show connotations (which reveal themselves generally to be ideological matters) connected with them. For example, he notes in a
discussion of toys in France:

> French toys *always mean something,* and this something is always
> entirely socialized, constituted by the myths or the techniques of
> modern adult life: the Army, Broadcasting, the Post Office, Medi-
> cine . . . School, Hair-Styling . . . , the Air Force (Parachutists), Trans-
> port (trains, Citroens, Vedettes, Vespas, petrol-stations), Science
> (Martian toys). (p. 53)

These "somethings" are the connotations of these objects, which Barthes explores in some detail, with brilliant stylistic flourishes and imaginative reaches. He does the same thing for Japanese culture in *Empire of Signs* (1977, 1982).

We can make an analogy with Saussurean semiological theory here. In a sense, we can suggest that denotation is the signifier and connotation is the signified, recognizing, however, that one signifier can have many signifieds. From Peirce's perspective, connotation would involve the realm of the symbolic, in which conventions are crucial. The meaning of the symbol has to be learned, and a given symbol can have many different meanings. The process of condensation is also relevant here. An image in a dream can be made of many different images or parts of images, and the connection of these different images to one image is similar in nature to the process of connotation.

Denotation

Denotation involves taking terms literally (including images, sounds, objects, or other forms of communication), in contrast to connotation, which involves looking at the various meanings a term carries with it or has given to it. Denotation deals with the literal meaning a sign conveys. Thus a Barbie Doll denotes a toy doll, first marketed in 1959, that was 11.5 inches high, had measurements of 5.25 inches at the bust, 3.0 inches at the waist, and 4.25 inches at the hips (these measurements have changed in recent years). What we have here is a literal description of a Barbie Doll and no more. What Barbie Dolls connote is another matter, about which there are many different views. For example, some scholars have suggested that the introduction and subsequent great popularity of the doll (and others like it) mark the end of motherhood as a dominant role for little girls in the United States, because Barbie spends her time as a "courtesan," buying clothes and having relationships with Ken and other dolls. She does not prepare little girls to be mothers, as earlier dolls did, dolls the girls could treat as babies, imitating their mothers' roles. A great

TABLE 4.3 Comparison of Denotation and Connotation

Denotation	Connotation
literal	figurative
signifier	signified(s)
evident	inferred
describes	suggests meaning
realm of existence	realm of myth

deal of criticism involves examining the connotations of objects, characters, and images and tying these meanings to historical, cultural, ideological, and other concerns.

We turn now to a discussion of metaphor and metonymy, which noted linguist Roman Jakobson suggests are fundamental ways of generating meaning. (I list Jakobson as an American in Table 1.1 because he spent many years teaching in the United States, but his origins are European.)

Metaphor

Metaphors are figures of speech that communicate meaning by analogy, by explaining or interpreting one thing in terms of something else (e.g., "My love is a red rose"). Similes also communicate by analogy, but in a weaker form that uses *like* or *as* (e.g., "My love is like a red rose"). Many people learn about metaphor in literature classes, where metaphor and simile are described as "figurative" language, and assume that metaphors are used only for poetic or literary purposes. They assume that metaphor is a relatively unimportant phenomenon. George Lakoff and Mark Johnson (1980) argue to the contrary; they see metaphors as central to our thinking:

> Most people think they can get along perfectly well without metaphor. We have found, on the contrary, that metaphor is pervasive in everyday life, not just in language but in thought and action. Our ordinary conceptual system, in terms of which we both think and act, is fundamentally metaphoric in nature.

The concepts that govern our thought are not just matters of the intellect. They also govern our everyday functioning down to the most mundane details. Our concepts structure what we perceive, how we get around in the world, and how we relate to other people. Our conceptual system thus plays a central role in defining our everyday realities. (p. 3)

Metaphor, then, plays an important role in the way we think and pervades our thinking. It is not just a literary device used by poets and other writers to generate certain kinds of emotional responses; it is a fundamental part of the way humans think and communicate.

Lakoff and Johnson discuss a number of different kinds of metaphors. Among them are the following:

- *structural* metaphors, which shape how we think, perceive, and act
- *orientational* metaphors, which deal with spatial orientation, as reflected in polar oppositions
- *ontological* metaphors, which interpret life in terms of common objects and substances

We often use verbs metaphorically, as in the following: The ship *sliced* (the ship is a knife or is like a knife) through the waves. We could substitute other verbs—*raced, cut, tore,* or something else—and in each case a different meaning would be conveyed. Metaphor, then, is not limited to the figurative language one finds in poetry; rather, it is a fundamental means of generating meaning. The same applies to metonymy, which is discussed in the next section.

Metonymy

Metonymy is a figure of speech in which meaning is communicated by association, in contrast to metaphor, where meaning is communicated by analogy. The term *metonymy* is composed of two parts: *meta*, or transfer, and *onoma*, or name. Thus, literally speaking, metonymy is "substitute naming."

TABLE 4.4 Comparison of Metaphor and Metonymy

Metaphor	Metonymy
analogy/similarity	association/contiguity
selection	combination
simile	synecdoche
romanticism	realism
surrealism (in paintings)	cubism (in paintings)
poetry	prose
Freud's identification and symbolism (in dreams)	Freud's condensation and displacement (in dreams)

In an essay of considerable theoretical importance (and difficulty) on aphasia—a disease associated with brain damage that
prevents people from expressing ideas—Roman Jakobson (1988)
discusses the difference between metaphor and metonymy:

> Every form of aphasic disturbance consists in some impairment, more
> or less severe, either of the faculty for selection and substitution or
> for combination and contexture. The former affliction involves a
> deterioration of metalinguistic operations, while the latter damages
> the capacity for maintaining the hierarchy of linguistic units. The
> relation of similarity is suppressed in the former, the relation of
> contiguity in the latter type of aphasia. Metaphor is alien to the
> similarity disorder, and metonymy to the contiguity disorder.
>   The development of a discourse may take place along two different
> semantic lines: one topic may lead to another either through their
> similarity or through their contiguity. The metaphoric way would
> be the most appropriate for the first case and the metonymic way
> for the second, since they find their most condensed expression in
> metaphor and metonymy respectively. (pp. 57-58)

We have, then, two polarities: metaphor and metonymy. Metaphor communicates by selection (a focus on the similarity between
things) and metonymy by combination (a focus on the association in time and space between things). Simile is a weaker form
of metaphor (using *like* or *as*) and synecdoche is a weaker form
of metonymy (in which a part stands for the whole, or vice versa).
These differences (and a number of others, drawn from other sections of Jakobson's article) are shown in Table 4.4.

According to Jakobson, one can determine a writer's style based on how he or she uses these two rhetorical devices and which of these "poles" prevails. The distinction has relevance for any symbolic process, as Jakobson (1988) explains:

> A competition between both devices, metonymic and metaphoric, is manifest in any symbolic process, be it interpersonal or social. Thus in an inquiry into the structure of dreams, the decisive question is whether the symbols and the temporal sequences are based on contiguity (Freud's metonymic "displacement" and synecdochic "condensation") or on similarity (Freud's "identification" and "symbolism"). (p. 60)

It is relatively easy to analyze metaphors, Jakobson adds, but dealing with metonymy is much more difficult, and the process, which he says "easily defies interpretation," has been relatively neglected.

What makes things even more complicated is that we frequently find the two processes mixed up together. Thus an image of a snake in a painting or advertisement can function metaphorically as a phallic symbol and metonymically as suggesting the snake in the Garden of Eden. This reference to Eden has a historic aspect to it, which leads us to our next set of concepts, synchronic analysis and diachronic analysis.

Synchronic Analysis and Diachronic Analysis

Ferdinand de Saussure (1966) makes a distinction between static (synchronic) and evolutionary (diachronic) linguistics, a distinction that we now apply to modes of analyzing texts and cultural phenomena:

> All sciences would profit by indicating more precisely the co-ordinates along which their subject matter is aligned. Everywhere distinctions should be made . . . between (1) *the axis of simultaneities* . . . , which stands for the relations of coexisting things and from which the intervention of time is excluded; and (2) *the axis of*

TABLE 4.5 Comparison of Synchronic Analysis and Diachronic Analysis

Synchronic Analysis	Diachronic Analysis
simultaneity	succession
instant in time	historical perspective
relations in a system	relations in time
analysis the focus	development the focus
static	evolutionary

> *successions* . . . , on which only one thing can be considered at a time
> but upon which are located all the things on the first axis together
> with their changes. (pp. 79-80)

Saussure further explains the difference between these two
perspectives by suggesting that we imagine a plant. If we make
a longitudinal cut in the stem of the plant, we see the fibers that
"constitute the plant" (p. 87), but if we make a transverse cut
(that is, a cross-sectional cut), we see the fibers in a certain relationship to one another—which we do not see when we look at the
longitudinal cut. Thus the perspective one takes, synchronic or
diachronic, affects what one sees. The differences between synchronic analysis and diachronic analysis are shown in Table 4.5.
A person cannot deal with something from both synchronic and
diachronic perspectives at the same time, Saussure adds, but both
perspectives are necessary. Saussure makes this distinction as part
of an argument for studying linguistics from a synchronic as well
as a diachronic perspective.

Let us consider how the distinction between synchronic analysis and diachronic analysis applies to the study of media and
popular culture. A person can focus on the way a given phenomenon, such as MTV or rap music, has evolved, or he or she can focus
on the phenomenon at a given point in time, or he or she can use
one perspective and then the other—but one person cannot take
both perspectives at the same time. This notion that the two approaches are mutually exclusive is similar to the figure and ground
phenomenon involved in an often-seen optical illusion: a picture
of two silhouetted profiles that can be seen instead as the silhou-
ette of a vase. One can look either at the figure and see the vase

or at the ground and see the faces, but one cannot see both at the same time.

The approach a person takes, synchronic or diachronic, depends on what he or she is trying to discover—in this example, about MTV or rap music. If taking the synchronic view, the person would look at MTV or rap at a given point in time and try to relate it to cultural, social, and political matters. If taking the diachronic perspective, he or she would examine the way MTV or rap has evolved over the years, important figures in MTV or rap, and that kind of thing. Another way an investigator might look at rap music involves its relation to other forms of African American expression, such as the doubles, in which case he or she would be looking at it in terms of its historical connections.

Intertextuality

There is a considerable amount of controversy about what intertextuality is and how it should be defined. (This applies also to many other concepts and theories used by cultural critics, I might add.) This concept is generally defined as the suggestion that all texts are (to varying degrees) related to one another because of our common cultural heritage, and, in some cases, that texts actually make use of plots, characters, events, themes, heroes and heroines, and stylistic devices found in texts that preceded them. Intertextuality, then, involves the use in texts, either consciously (through "quotation") or unconsciously, of material from other texts (this topic was dealt with briefly in Chapter 2, in the discussion of Bakhtin's notion of dialogism).

Parody is a good example of intertextuality. There are three kinds of parody, or comic imitation: parody of specific works, parody of the distinctive styles of particular authors or creative artists, and parody of particular genres. Parodies are best appreciated when we are familiar with what is being parodied, though they can be very funny and still be appreciated without a knowledge of the work, style, or genre being parodied. For example, the film *Der Dove* is an extremely funny parody of the style of

Ingmar Bergman; it uses Bergmanesque characters who speak in broad mock Swedish, has a Bergmanesque plot, spoofs Bergman's filmic style, and so on. Many people find it extremely funny, but people who have seen such Bergman films as *Wild Strawberries* and *The Seventh Seal* can enjoy it even more.

Parody represents a conscious "quotation" (and manipulation) of a text, genre, or literary or creative style—that is, of someone else's work. In some cases, writers and other kinds of artists draw upon important themes that many people are familiar with. Thus the film *Forbidden Planet* is based on Shakespeare's *The Tempest*, and many films and television programs use plots and themes from folkloristic sources—all examples of intertextuality. Other examples include the musical play *Kiss Me Kate* and Shakespeare's *Taming of the Shrew* and the musical play *West Side Story* and Shakespeare's *Romeo and Juliet*. In these cases, the intertextuality is obvious, and the authors of the musical plays consciously used Shakespeare for their source—though they made many modifications. But in many cases intertextuality is not so obvious, and authors do not recognize that they are duplicating (in modified form) plots, themes, characters, and so on that have been used before.

The phenomenon of intertextual borrowing is not new. As Bakhtin (1981) points out in a discussion of the Middle Ages:

> The role of the other's word was enormous at that time: there were quotations that were openly and reverently emphasized as such, or that were half-hidden, half-conscious, unconscious, correct, intentionally distorted, unintentionally distorted, deliberately reinterpreted and so forth. . . . One of the best authorities on medieval parody . . . states outright that the history of medieval literature and its Latin literature in particular "is the history of appropriation, re-working and imitation of someone else's property." (p. 69)

From Bakhtin's perspective, intertextuality is rooted in the dialogical way that people communicate, a topic discussed in Chapter 2. In conversation/dialogue, what we say is dependent on what others have said and are saying and what we anticipate they will say. Our conversation is dialogical, and, by extension, so is our creativity.

Auteur Theory

As the term suggests, an *auteur* is an author, someone whose aesthetic sensibilities and impact are most important in the creation of a text. With literary texts, discerning authorship is usually no problem. But with collaborative art forms, such as film, deciding on authorship is much more complicated. Generally speaking, film theorists have concluded that it is the director of a film who is the auteur, the most important creative figure.

But auteur theory is concerned with more than one film; it is concerned with the work of a director—with his or her whole corpus of films, and with certain dominant themes and stylistic aspects of these films. The text in auteur criticism is not one film, but the body of work of the director. Peter Wollen (1973) explains auteur theory as follows:

> The great directors must be defined in terms of shifting relations, in their singularity as well as their uniformity. Renoir once remarked that a director spends his whole life making one film; this film, which it is the task of the critic to construct, consists not only of the typical features of its variants, which are merely its redundancies, but of the principle of variation which governs it, that is its esoteric structure, which can only manifest itself or "seep to the surface," in Lévi-Strauss's phrase, "through the repetition process." (p. 104)

Auteur critics, as Wollen suggests, not only look for common themes, but search for the principles (often not apparent) that generate these themes and numerous stylistic and other variations on them. That is, the auteur critic looks for the structure underlying a corpus of films, so auteur criticism is therefore an a posteriori (after-the-fact) kind of criticism. Once the critic discovers this structure, he or she can then analyze particular films in terms of how they relate to this structure or, to put it another way, the codes or aesthetic and stylistic principles underlying the body of films. Among the concerns of an auteur critic of film, Wollen adds, would be such matters as visual style, tempo, recurring motifs, and thematic preoccupations. There are also other concerns or techniques critics can use when they analyze texts, including syntagmatic analysis and paradigmatic analysis, to which we now turn.

Syntagmatic Analysis

The term *syntagm* means chain, and the syntagmatic analysis of texts involves the study of the linear progression of narratives. Editing, in essence, involves manipulating the order of elements in a text to generate meaning and to trigger certain kinds of responses in the audiences of texts. This applies to everything from word order in literary works to the progression of images (shots, for example) in films, a topic dealt with in Chapter 2, in the discussion of montage.

Vladimir Propp, a Russian folklorist, wrote a pioneering text in 1928 titled *The Morphology of the Folktale,* in which he analyzes a number of Russian folktales and suggests that all of them can be understood in terms of a limited number of functions—that is, acts of their characters in terms of their significance for the action:

> For the sake of comparison we shall separate the component parts of fairy tales by special methods; and then, we shall make a comparison of the tales according to their components. The result will be a morphology (i.e., a description of the tale according to its component parts and the relationship of these components to each other and to the whole). (Propp, 1928/1968, p. 19)

Propp decided to use functions for analysis because, he argues, there is no logical way to deal with themes in stories, because different analysts use different classification methods to analyze them.

Functions, Propp suggests, are the fundamental components of a tale; in addition, he argues that the number of functions is limited, the sequence in which they are found is always identical, and all fairy tales of one type are the same as far as their structure is concerned. Propp's functions are shown in Table 4.6, which illustrates that many contemporary narrative texts—films, television programs, novels, comic strips, and so on—are modernizations of fairy tales and contain many of their elements. Even some texts that are not overtly narratives, such as television news shows, can be analyzed in terms of Proppian functions as well.

When we use Propp's functions in analyzing modern texts, we have to update and modify some of them. Thus at the end of contemporary texts the hero may sleep with the heroine. This is a modern variation on Propp's function that shows the hero marrying the princess in traditional Russian fairy tales. And we do not have to assume that the order of all texts will be the same, as Propp suggests. What is interesting is the degree to which Propp's morphology can be used to interpret contemporary texts—everything from James Bond films to national news programs on television.

Paradigmatic Analysis

Paradigmatic analysis, in the context of this discussion, involves the analysis of texts in terms of the patterns of opposition (based on the speech and actions of characters) found in texts. We can derive our means of determining the paradigmatic structure of texts from several sources. Saussure (1966) argues that concepts are defined differentially and take their meaning "not by their positive content but negatively from their relations with the other terms in the system" (p. 117).

We can apply Saussure's insight in looking at characters and can determine patterns of opposition between characters (such as heroes and villains) and between their actions (such as rescue a damsel in distress and kidnap a damsel). Claude Lévi-Strauss (1967) analyzed myths in terms of their elementary components or "mythemes"; he arranged these mythemes into patterns of opposition that reveal, he asserts, the hidden meaning of texts. We can adapt Lévi-Strauss's methodology and look for a set of

TABLE 4.6 Propp's 31 Functions of Characters

Function		Description	
	α	initial situation	Members of family are introduced; hero is introduced.
1.	β	absentation	One of the members of the family absents him- or herself.
2.	γ	interdiction	Interdiction is addressed to hero (can be reversed).
3.	δ	violation	Interdiction is violated.
4.	ε	reconnaissance	Villain makes attempt to get information.
5.	ζ	delivery	Villain gets information about victim.
6.	η	trickery	Villain tries to deceive victim.
7.	θ	complicity	Victim is deceived.
8.	A	villainy	Villain causes harm to a member of the family; or
	a	lack	member of the family lacks something, desires something.
9.	B	mediation	Misfortune made known; hero is dispatched.
10.	C	counteraction	Hero (seeker) agrees to, decides on counteraction.
11.	↑	departure	Hero leaves home.
12.	D	1st donor function	Hero tested, receives magical agent or helper.
13.	E	hero's reaction	Hero reacts to agent or donor.
14.	F	receipt of agent	Hero acquires use of magical agent.
15.	G	spatial change	Hero let to object of search.
16.	H	struggle	Hero and villain join in direct combat.
17.	J	branding	Hero is branded.
18.	I	victory	Villain is defeated.
19.	K	liquidation	Initial misfortune or lack is liquidated.
20.	↓	return	Hero returns.
21.	Pr	pursuit, chase	Hero is pursued.
22.	Rs	rescue	Hero is rescued from pursuit.
23.	O	unrecognized arrival	Hero, unrecognized, arrives home or elsewhere.
24.	L	unfounded claims	False hero presents unfounded claims.
25.	M	difficult task	Difficult task is proposed to hero.
26.	N	solution	The task is resolved.
27.	R	recognition	The hero is recognized.
28.	Ex	exposure	The false hero or villain is exposed.
29.	T	transfiguration	The hero is given a new appearance.
30.	U	punishment	The villain is punished.
31.	W	wedding	The hero is married, ascends the throne.

binary oppositions that inform a text, even though this may involve a certain amount of simplification. These can be put into a table listing polar oppositions, which can then be explained in some detail.

In making this table, we must find a basic, fundamental opposition in the text and then list characters, actions, events, dialogue spoken, and the like that line up logically and are related to one another under each of the oppositions. This analysis, according to Lévi-Strauss, can tell us the latent meaning or hidden meaning of a text. Syntagmatic analysis tells us what happens in a text; paradigmatic analysis tells what a text means, and often this is not apparent. What a paradigmatic analysis of a text reveals, in essence, is the way the human mind, below our level of awareness and with computerlike speed, makes sense of characters and their actions in texts. In making such a table, one must find real oppositions (happy, sad) and not simple negations (happy, not happy).

Meaning in texts, we must remember, always has to be elicited. It is not always apparent, and critics using different methodologies and perspectives will often find different meanings in texts. This matter of eliciting meaning is discussed in more detail below.

Structuralism

Structuralism is a method of analysis, based on linguistic theory and anthropological thought, that focuses on the relationships that exist among elements in a system instead of on the elements themselves. The system could be a myth, a novel, a film, a genre, literature in general, what you will. Jonathan Culler (1975), who discusses structuralism and its relation to semiotics, explains that cultural and social phenomena have meaning and therefore can be seen as signs, and that they are defined by internal and external networks of relationships, not essences:

> Stress may fall on one or the other of these propositions—it would be in these terms, for example, that one might try to distinguish semiology and structuralism—but in fact the two are inseparable,

> for in studying signs one must investigate the system of relations
> that enables meaning to be produced and, reciprocally, one can only
> determine what are the pertinent relations among items by consid-
> ering them as signs.
>   Structuralism is thus based, in the first instance, on the realization
> that if human actions or productions have a meaning there must be
> an underlying system of distinctions and conventions which makes
> this meaning possible. (p. 4)

Actions, events, and objects have meaning in relation to the culture
in which they are found (which suggests that their meaning is
conventional or arbitrary, and not natural), and this culture may
be looked upon as a system of signs and conventions or rules for
interpreting these signs. We can see, then, a connection between
this kind of thinking and the work of Saussure, who I quoted
earlier to the effect that concepts are essentially differential and
are not understood on the basis of their positive content but
negatively by their relations with other terms.

When it comes to the structural analysis of a literary text, we
can adapt the techniques used by Lévi-Strauss in his analyses of
myths. He suggests, let us recall, that a myth is, in effect, a system
composed of various actions of characters, or elementary units
called "mythemes." In a celebrated study of the myth of Oedipus,
Lévi-Strauss (1967) arranged the mythemes into bundles of relations that he saw as the "true constituent units" of the myth;
these bundles yielded insights into the real and previously unrecognized meaning of this myth.

The modification to Lévi-Strauss's technique that I propose is
based on the fact that human thinking is, as Jakobson has suggested, binary in nature. As Culler (1975) puts it, "Structuralists
have generally followed Jakobson and taken the binary opposition as a fundamental operation of the human mind basic to the
production of meaning" (p. 15). In doing a structuralist analysis
of a text, then, we look for the sets of paired polar oppositions
that give meaning to the text. This is best done by creating a table
listing the oppositions and then explaining what the oppositions
reveal in the body of an essay. It is important to remember that

TABLE 4.7 Polar Oppositions in *Upstairs, Downstairs*

Upstairs	Downstairs
wealthy	poor
masters (command)	servants (obey)
leisure	hard work
do stupid things	shrewd
champagne	beer
marriage (and infidelity)	bachelorhood/spinsterhood

we seek real oppositions, not simple negations. The oppositions are linked horizontally in that they are paired, and vertically in that all the elements on one side of the table should be tied to one another.

As an example, let's look at the British television series *Upstairs, Downstairs*, which has recently returned (as of spring 1994) to Public Broadcasting. Table 4.7 displays some polar oppositions one might find in the series in general (one could make similar lists about each episode of the series). In the table, each of the items listed under "upstairs" is the opposite of a corresponding item listed under "downstairs," and all of the items in each column are connected to one another. Of course, not many texts offer their binary opposites in their titles, but in this case, had the series instead been called *The Bellamys*, our chart of polar oppositions would still be the same, involving those living upstairs and those living downstairs.

This table represents a paradigmatic analysis of the text of *Upstairs, Downstairs* and reflects the latent meaning of the text. According to Lévi-Strauss, let us recall, a paradigmatic analysis of a text reveals the text's hidden meaning, whereas a syntagmatic analysis, using Propp's functions, for example, essentially tells us what happens in the text. We know from reception theorists that texts are infinitely complex, and that readers play an important role in interpreting texts, but that does not mean that texts have no internal or hidden structures of oppositions that give them meaning, or that some readings of texts are not better than others.

Conclusion

Semiotics and semiology focus our attention on how people generate meanings—in their use of language, in their behavior (body language, dress, facial expression, and so on), and in creative texts of all kinds. Everyone tries to make sense of human behavior, in our everyday lives, in the novels we read, in the films and television shows we see, in the concerts we attend, in sports events we watch or participate in—humans are meaning-generating and meaning-interpreting animals, whatever else we are. We are always sending messages and always receiving and interpreting the messages others send us. What semiotics and semiology do is provide us with more refined and sophisticated ways of interpreting these messages—and of sending them. In particular, they provide us with methods of analyzing texts in cultures and cultures as texts.

Sigmund Freud

5

Psychoanalytic Theory and Cultural Criticism

In this chapter I will explain a number of the fundamental conceptions found in psychoanalytic theory, which is one of the most important methodologies used by cultural critics. My focus will be on the ideas of Sigmund Freud, but I will also deal with a number of concepts associated with Jungian analysis.

Psychoanalytic theory is, it must be said, extremely controversial; there are some scholars and critics who feel that Freudian, Jungian, and other psychoanalytic theories are absurd and have no relevance either to human beings or to cultural phenomena. On the other hand, Freudian thought, along with Jungian thought and the ideas of numerous other psychoanalytic thinkers, is used by a significant number of cultural critics and seems to have a number of interesting things to say about texts, media, popular culture, and related matters. Many observers, including poet W. H. Auden, have noted that Freudian thought is so pervasive in Western societies that many people use Freud's ideas without even recognizing that they come from Freud or from thinkers associated with him. With that in mind, let us examine some of Freud's more important ideas.

The Unconscious

One of Freud's most fundamental ideas involves the notion that the psyche has a number of different levels or systems of awareness: consciousness, preconsciousness, and the unconscious. This is known as Freud's *topographic* hypothesis. In L. Hinsie and R. J. Campbell's *Psychiatric Dictionary* (1970) these systems are differentiated. Consciousness refers, generally speaking, to what we are aware of. It is a "proportionately infinitesimal" part of the psyche. The other two levels are described as follows:

> preconscious . . . in psychoanalysis, one of the three topographical divisions of the psyche. . . . The preconscious division includes thought, memories and similar mental elements which although not conscious at the moment, can readily be brought into consciousness . . . by an effort of attention. This is in contrast to the unconscious . . . division, whose elements are barred from access to consciousness by some intrapsychic force such as repression. (p. 585)

These three levels can be represented metaphorically by an iceberg (see Figure 5.1). The part of the iceberg that appears above the water is comparable to the consciousness. What can be seen immediately below the water, if we look carefully, corresponds to what Freud calls preconsciousness. And what is hidden in the murky depths of the sea, and is infinitely larger than the visible part of the iceberg, is the unconscious.

The unconscious is important, for purposes of this discussion, because many of the important elements in texts are connected to unconscious processes in the creators of these texts and in ourselves, when we read or see or listen to these texts. Psychoanalytic critics generally hold that

> because both neurosis and creative writing are related to daydreaming, Freud . . . attempted to exploit the connection to throw some light on certain aspects of creative writing. Since his pioneering work it has become abundantly evident that the same unconscious, instinctual wishes and conflicts that play so large a part in the production

consciousness
preconsciousness
unconscious

Figure 5.1. Freud's Topographic Hypothesis as Iceberg

of dreams and daydreams are equally responsible for literary productions. That is to say, a writer fashions his daydreams, his fantasy,
into a form which he hopes will be interesting—in the broadest sense,
enjoyable—to other people. Daydreaming, in general, is for oneself.
Writing, in general, is for an audience. (Brenner, 1974, pp. 229-230)

In understanding the power of texts, we must be aware of the
way they are tied to elements in our unconscious, which explains
why texts are generally so difficult to interpret.

There is probably some kind of a communication between the
unconscious of the writer (and creative artists in all media) and
the unconscious of the reader (or member of an audience). Neither the creator nor the audience member understands or is
aware of what is going on, which explains, in part, why we can't
ask authors what their works mean.

Freud developed another theory of the psyche as well, called
the *structural* hypothesis, which explains consciousness in terms
of elements in the psyche called the id, the ego, and the superego.
It is to these components of this hypothesis (which also help us
understand texts and creative activity in general) that we now turn.

The Id

In Freud's structural hypothesis, the id is generally recognized as the psychic representative of the drives. It stands in contrast to the superego, which represents conscience and moral beliefs. Freud (1933) describes the id in graphic terms:

> We can come nearer to the id with images, and call it chaos, a cauldron of seething excitement. We suppose that it is somewhere in direct contact with somatic process, and takes over from them instinctual needs and gives them mental representation. These instincts fill it with energy, but it has no organization and no unified will, only an impulsion to obtain satisfaction for the instinctual needs, in accordance with the pleasure-principle. (quoted in Hinsie & Campbell, 1970, p. 362)

The id is a source of energy, and must not be held in check too much. At the same time, it must be contained, for those whose id is not controlled are unable to defer gratification in order to educate themselves, plan for the future, and function as responsible individuals in society. Such people's lives are dominated by their impulses.

According to Freud, the id constitutes the total psychic apparatus of the newborn; the psyche later then splits into three parts, adding an ego and a superego. Other theorists disagree with the notion that the psyche is all id at birth, but it is generally held that the id precedes the development of the ego and superego. The ego is held to start functioning early in life, perhaps at around 6 months of age, and is concerned with the environment, because the ego is involved in making sure that the id secures its gratifications.

The Ego

The ego is held to be the "executant" of the drives and, in serving this function, it generally mediates between the id and the superego, trying to keep them in balance. According to Hinsie and Campbell (1970):

> In psychoanalytic psychology, the ego is that part of the psychic apparatus which is the mediator between the person and reality. Its prime function is the perception of reality and adaptation to it. . . . The various tasks of the ego include: perception, including self-perception and self-awareness; motor control (action); adaptation to reality; use of the reality principle. (p. 247)

As noted above, the concepts of the id, the ego, and the superego make up Freud's structural hypothesis, in contrast to his earlier topographical hypothesis, which focuses on consciousness, pre-consciousness, and the unconscious.

In cultural analysis, we can often find figures in texts who can be described as ego figures, or figures whose functions are essentially ego functions—dealing with an individual's relationship to his or her environment. (We can also find id figures, who are motivated primarily by the desire for pleasure, and superego figures, who represent conscience and related matters.) In the same manner, we can find objects, institutions, and other phenomena that essentially represent or reflect the ego. The ego defends itself, from anxieties and other attacks, by using a number of "defense mechanisms," such as repression, denial, ambivalence, displacement, and projection.

The Superego

The superego deserves a bit more attention than the id and the ego in this discussion. According to Freud, the superego is the agency in our psyches involved with conscience, morality, and ideal aspirations. Charles Brenner (1974) describes the superego as having the following functions:

> 1. the approval or disapproval of actions and wishes on the grounds of rectitude. 2. critical self-observation. 3. self-punishment. 4. the demand of reparation or repentance for wrong-doing. 5. self-praise or self-love as a reward for virtuous or desirable thoughts and actions. Contrary to the ordinary meaning of "conscience," however, we understand that the functions of the superego are often largely or completely unconscious. (pp. 111-112)

The superego functions, then, in opposition to the id. What is interesting, as Brenner points out, is that our superegos are shaped primarily by the superegos of our grandparents. They are responsible for shaping the superegos of our parents, who, in turn, train us and give us our moral sensibilities. And, Brenner adds, the severity of our superegos is not tied to the severity of the training our parents give us, but to the way they have dealt with their Oedipus complexes and our internalization of this process. The superego develops, originally, according to psychoanalytic theory, out of our need to repudiate hostile wishes we have, basically incestuous in nature, which may be described as our Oedipus complexes.

We identify, so this theory goes, with the superegos of our parents when they were wrestling with their Oedipus complexes. Thus we identify with our parents' superegos, which are formed in great part by their parents. Disapproval by our superegos leads to feelings of guilt and remorse; approval leads to feelings of joy and satisfaction.

Freud also used the concept of the superego to explain the power that leaders and charismatic figures have over people. This analysis applies to political organizations, sects, cults, and so on. What happens, Freud suggested, is that people identify with their leaders, and the images of these leaders become "a part of the superego of each of the members of the group" (Brenner, 1974, p. 124). Thus the members of the group are united by sharing, so to speak, the superego of the leader.

The Oedipus Complex

The Oedipus complex is one of Freud's most controversial and most resonant ideas. In a celebrated letter to Wilhelm Fliess written October 15, 1897, Freud explains how he developed the concept of the Oedipus complex:

> Being entirely honest with oneself is a good exercise. Only one idea of general value has occurred to me. I have found love of the

mother and jealousy of the father in my own case too, and now believe it to be a general phenomena of early childhood, even if it
does not always occur so early as in children who have been made
hysterics. . . . If that is the case, the gripping power of *Oedipus Rex*,
in spite of all the rational objections to the inexorable fate that the
story presupposes, becomes intelligible, and one can understand
why later fate dramas were such failures. Our feelings rise against
any arbitrary individual fate . . . but the Greek myth seizes on a
compulsion which everyone recognizes because he has felt traces
of it in himself. Every member of the audience was once a budding
Oedipus in fantasy, and this dream-fulfillment played out in reality
causes everyone to recoil in horror, with the full measure of repression which separates his fantasy from his present state.

For Freud, the Oedipus complex is the central or "nuclear" core
of neuroses, and how we resolve our Oedipus complexes affects
the way we develop and whether we are relatively normal or become neurotic. And, as we have seen, it affects the way our children
develop also.

Freud argued that the Oedipus complex is found in everyone
because it is natural and not environmental. There is a divergence
of opinion among anthropologists as to whether this is correct,
but there is evidence that seems to suggest it is and that the Oedipus
complex is found everywhere. (There is also an inverse or negative Oedipus complex, which involves fantasies of incest with the
parent of the same sex and murderous wishes toward the parent
of the opposite sex.)

The Oedipus complex is normally resolved or mastered; in little
boys this is done through the agency of castration anxiety (the
fear that the father will castrate the boy) and in little girls through
penis envy (the fantasy girls have that they have lost their penises). Castration anxiety, so the theory goes, leads boys to identify with their fathers' masculinity and to renounce their love for
their mothers. This masculinity is then channeled into love outside of the confines of the family and toward other women. Penis
envy leads girls to reidentify with their mothers and turn to males
(other than their fathers) to obtain babies, and, indirectly, their
"lost" penises. These concepts are, of course, controversial, and
many people find them utterly absurd. Freudians would argue

that such scoffers are repressing their instinctual wishes—repression being the most important defense mechanism of the ego.

The female equivalent of the Oedipus complex is often called the Electra complex, after the myth of Electra, daughter of Agamemnon. Electra induced her brother Orestes to kill their mother, Clytemnestra, and her new husband, in retribution for their having killed Agamemnon. Electra refused to marry and brooded endlessly over the death of her father. This story reminds one of *Hamlet* (except that the sexes are reversed), and, in fact, Freud speculated that the Oedipus complex is at the root of *Hamlet* (Ernest Jones has written a book on this subject titled *Hamlet and Oedipus,* 1949).

There are several other complexes related to the Oedipus complex that are worth noting. The Heracles complex involves a father who hates his children and wishes to do away with them because he sees them as rivals for the affection of his wife. The Jocasta complex (named after the mother of Oedipus) involves a mother who is overly attached (in some cases incestuously attached) to her son.

Brenner (1974) goes so far as to argue that the Oedipus complex is at the heart of all literature, "for a literary work to have a strong, or, even more, a lasting appeal, its plot must arouse and gratify some important aspect of the unconscious oedipal wishes of the members of its audience" (p. 235). The characters in literary works—and we can expand this to mean texts found in the mass media, such as television and film—often represent disguised versions of parental figures and their sons and daughters, but unless there is some kind of resonance with repressed childhood instinctual wishes, the work, Brenner suggests, has little impact.

In the same light, comedy can be seen as involving a reversal of the Oedipal relationship. Martin Grotjahn (1966) explains:

Comedy has been considered a low form of artistic creation. It has aroused little analytic interest. The only exception is a work by Ludwig Jekels written almost thirty years ago, "The Origin of the Comedy."

The thesis is simple, straightforward, and convincing: the tragic guilt of the son is displaced upon the father. In comedy it is the father who is guilty. This inversion of guilt can be seen in Shakespeare's classic comedies as in all others. The villain is the victim of his own villainy; the cheat is cheated. . . . The son plays the role of the father and the father is cast in the role of the son. The result is amused superiority, laughing aggression, triumph without remorse, guilt, or fear of punishment. (p. 87)

This "reversed" Oedipus situation is found in our lives, Grotjahn adds, for as we grow old we find younger people taking over and we become more or less irrelevant and, in a way, comic characters.

The Oedipus complex, Grotjahn suggests, is "the cornerstone of all culture as we know it" (p. 260); it informs our expressive works, both tragic and comic. It helps us work through our unconscious problems and conflicts, both as individuals and as collectivities; as such, it plays a much more profound role in our lives than we may possibly imagine.

We now turn to two other processes that are of significance in our mental lives and in our expressive works: condensation and displacement.

Condensation

Condensation refers to the representation of a number of ideas or images by a single word or image—or even a fragment of an idea or image. The process is one in which one thing, a word, a symbol, an image, has many different meanings.

In *The Interpretation of Dreams*, Freud (1965) distinguishes between the manifest and latent content of dreams. The manifest content of dreams, what he calls "dream content," is what we remember of our dreams; the latent content, what he calls "dream thoughts," has to be interpreted from the dream content. The relationship between dream content and dream thoughts is of great interest to Freud:

The first thing that becomes clear to anyone who compares the dream-content with the dream-thoughts is that a work of *condensation* on a large scale has been carried out. Dreams are brief, meagre and laconic in comparison with the range and wealth of dream-thoughts. If a dream is written out it may perhaps fill half a page. The analysis setting out the dream-thoughts underlying it may occupy six, eight or a dozen times as much space. (pp. 312-313)

This is because a process of condensation has taken place in which elements of different things are unified or "condensed" into one thing, or one idea can contain the emotions connected with a number of different ideas.

Condensation involves combination. Because one item may mean many different things, telling what happened in a dream might be done rather quickly, but figuring out what the dream means is much more difficult. In fact, Freud suggests that because of condensation, one can never be sure a dream is interpreted completely; there may be meanings hidden behind the meanings that are elicited in the analysis.

The process of condensation is not unique to dreams; we find condensation in many works of expressive art, including print advertisements and radio and television commercials. The French thinker Jacques Lacan (1966) suggests that condensation is essentially a metaphoric or analogical process, in that it links a number of seemingly different things together into some kind of unity.

Hinsie and Campbell (1970) explain the process of condensation as follows:

This process of emotional condensation is characteristic of almost all dreams. As Jones expresses it, a person in a dream "may be constituted by the fusion of the memories of several different actual persons." (Jones, E. *Papers on Psycho-Analysis*, 4th ed., Wood, Baltimore, 1938)

A second meaning of condensation is a corollary of the first. Many ideas or allied experiences may be compressed into a single thought or word. Thus a phobia is never an entity; it is representative of a chain of circumstances; it is a symbol that expresses a number of experiences. (p. 150)

It is this enormous depth that an image, idea, or symbol may have that makes condensation so powerful and, at the same time, so difficult to interpret when condensation is found in dreams and in expressive works. It is also condensation that gives dreams and expressive works their richness. Now we turn to another process found in dreams and expressive works, displacement, which works in tandem, we might say, with condensation.

Displacement

When we dream, according to Freud, we take liberties with our wishes and desires. We generate images that unite a number of ideas or images into one (condensation), and we also substitute acceptable (to our superegos, that is) images for unacceptable ones, a process Freud terms *displacement*. Erich Fromm (1957) describes this phenomenon:

> By displacement Freud refers to the fact that an element of the latent dream, and often a very important one, is expressed by a remote element in the manifest dream and usually one which appears to be quite unimportant. As a result, the manifest dream often treats the really important elements as if they were of no particular significance and thus disguises the true meaning of the dream. (pp. 70-71)

The true dream, Fromm explains, expresses our hidden desires and is what Freud calls the latent dream. The disguised or distorted version of this dream, as we remember it, is the manifest dream, and the process of distortion is called "dream work." The mechanisms dream work uses are condensation, displacement, and secondary elaboration.

Secondary elaboration refers to the process by which we fill in gaps, repair inconsistencies, and turn the latent dream into a coherent narrative. In dreams, Fromm adds, two other phenomena complicate things: First, elements frequently stand for their opposites; second, "the manifest dream does not express logical relations between its various elements. It has no 'but,' 'therefore,' 'because,' 'if,' but expresses these logical relations in the relation between the pictorial images" (p. 71).

Freud offers many interesting analyses of dreams in his writings. One of the most fascinating appears in an essay titled "The Occurrence in Dreams of Material from Fairy-Tales" (1963). In this dream, a young married woman dreams she is in a room that is entirely brown. A little door leads to the top of a steep staircase, and up this staircase comes a strange little manikin—"small, with white hair, a bald top to his head and a red nose." He is dressed in a gray garment through which his figure is visible. He dances around the room and carries on in a strange way.

Freud analyzes the sexual significance of the little man in the room as follows:

> The room, at this level, was the vagina. (The room was in her—this was reversed in the dream.) The little man who made grimaces and behaved so funnily was the penis. The narrow door and the steep stairs confirmed the view that the situation was a representation of coitus. (p. 61)

The gray garment (which was transparent) turns out to be a condom. It seems that the woman was anxiety-ridden about getting pregnant after having had relations with her husband. This story suggests the way we disguise things in our dreams.

In this particular dream, the act of sexual intercourse was displaced by a scene in which a little man danced around in a room. And a condom turned into a transparent gray garment. Freud offers interpretations of various other aspects of the dream that do not concern us at this moment. The point is that dreams are very complicated matters; analyzing them is always difficult, particularly because of the processes of condensation and displacement.

These processes are at work in our mass-mediated dreams as well, which is why Freud's theories about dreams are of such interest to many cultural critics. What Freud offers is an introduction to the analysis of symbolization and the process by which people find meaning in visual images and narratives of all kinds.

He is famous, or perhaps infamous is a better term, for his ideas about the relations between symbols and sexuality. Symbolism is important because it enables the ego to trick the superego, as it were, and help the id obtain desired gratifications.

According to Freud (1953):

> The male genital organ is symbolically represented in dreams in many different ways. . . . Its more conspicuous and, to both sexes, more interesting part, the penis, is symbolized primarily by objects which resemble it in form, being long and upstanding, such as *sticks, umbrellas, poles, trees* and the like; also by objects which, like the thing symbolized, have the property of penetration, and consequently of injuring the body,—that is to say pointed weapons of all sorts: *knives, daggers, lances, sabres*; firearms are similarly used: *guns, pistols and revolvers.* (pp. 160-161)

Freud adds to this list objects from which water flows (taps, watering cans), objects that are capable of elongation (pencils, pulley lamps, and hammers), and objects that can raise themselves upright, mirroring erections in males (balloons, airplanes, zeppelins). In some cases the organ of sex becomes a whole person, and we find dreamers flying. All of these symbols are connected, Freud adds, to wish fulfillment, and, more important, the wish of a man generally is to be with a woman, whether he is aware of it or not.

Freud moves on to symbols of women:

> The female genitalia are symbolically represented by all such objects as share with them the property of enclosing a space or are capable of acting as receptacles: such as *pits, hollows and caves,* and also *jars and bottles,* and *boxes* of all sorts and sizes, *chests, coffers, pockets,* and so forth. *Ships,* too, come into this category. Many symbols refer rather to the uterus than to the other genital organs: thus *cupboards, stoves,* and above all, *rooms.* Room symbolism here links up with that of houses, whilst *doors and gates* represent the genital opening. (pp. 163-164)

To this he adds other phenomena such as fruit, woods and thickets (symbolizing pubic hair), and jewel cases. Sexual intercourse is symbolically represented, he adds, by rhythmic activities, such as dancing, riding, and climbing, and by the experience of some kind of violence.

All of this material, Freud cautions, is connected to our dreams, where we are trying to outwit our superego dream censor. A famous remark attributed to Freud is often quoted when psychoanalytic critics deal with sexual symbolism in texts: "Sometimes a cigar is just a cigar." This is quite true, but it also suggests that *sometimes* a cigar is not just a cigar. Our knowledge of these symbols comes, Freud adds, from language, folktales, jokes, and myths. It is to one of the most important myths, from a psychoanalytic point of view, that we now turn.

Narcissism

The term *narcissism* comes from Narcissus, the name of a character in Greek mythology. Narcissus was a beautiful young man who attracted the attention of many young women, but, to the women's chagrin, he was indifferent to all of them. Echo, a nymph, fell in love with Narcissus, and he rejected her cruelly; as punishment for his unkindness, the gods condemned him to love only himself. One day, as Narcissus bent over a pool of water to take a drink, he saw his reflection in the water and fell in love with it. At that moment he recognized that how he now felt about himself, others had felt about him. He could not stop looking at his reflection; he pined away for love of himself and died on the bank of the pool, and where he died there bloomed a new flower, the narcissus.

Psychologists tell us that every person needs an element of narcissism, or self-love—that is, there is a healthy kind of narcissism, which leads to us to accomplish things and helps us to develop self-esteem. In its unhealthy manifestation, narcissism becomes a dominating factor in a person's life; a narcissistic individual sees him- or herself as superior to others, is exploitative and self-centered, craves constant adulation, becomes angered and moody when criticized, and becomes depressed by failures. Narcissists seem very self-assured on the surface, but underneath they are extremely anxiety-ridden and insecure.

Narcissism is most commonly discussed in relation to individuals, but it has social and political implications and can be found in collectivities as well. Freud suggested that individuals can focus their attention and energy (especially libidinal or sexual energy) in either of two directions: toward the outside world or toward the self. When we are very young, we naturally focus our energy on ourselves; as we grow older we learn, in most cases, to redirect it outward. Narcissists do not accomplish this redirection adequately.

Some psychologists suggest that the roots of narcissism develop when children are between 18 months and 3 years old. They theorize that if a child in this age group is not allowed to develop his or her own identity, and is attacked verbally and criticized by his or her parents, the child will feel there is something wrong with him or her, and may develop narcissistic patterns of behavior—grandiosity, a smug sense of superiority—to protect him- or herself from feelings of inadequacy.

Erich Fromm discusses narcissism in his book *The Greatness and Limitations of Freud's Thought* (1980), and he makes a number of interesting points. Narcissism, he suggests, does have a survival value. We have to feel that it is important that we look after ourselves, accomplish things, and so on. Fromm suggests that Freud's views on narcissism were distorted by his views of women and the nature of love. According to Fromm, Freud was unable to see narcissism as the opposite of love because he had mistaken ideas about the way men and women love each other; this stemmed, in part, from the class system and the way middle-class women were taught to behave.

Many narcissists are attractive individuals—Fromm (1980) suggests that "many artists and creative writers, dancers and politicians are extremely narcissistic" (p. 47)—and this narcissism does not interfere with their art, but actually helps it. These narcissists, according to Fromm, "portray an image of what the average person would like to be" (p. 47), and this is very appealing to the average person (who does not appreciate the anxiety that narcissists suffer).

Fromm also makes a distinction between narcissism and egoism. The latter refers to a kind of selfishness and greediness, which is different from the distorted view of reality found in the narcissist, who may not be an egoist but who is afflicted by self-love. Egoists may be selfish, but they can be realistic as well. Some narcissists direct their energies toward disguising their self-love; they take on a mask of humility and engage in clearly selfless behavior, such as performing humanitarian acts, as a means of masking their narcissism.

All of this makes it very difficult, generally speaking, to detect narcissism and deal with it. Narcissists do not tend to "bond" with therapists, and they resist treatment. There is a tendency in social thought to tie the terms together, and to explain egoism, an excessive concern with the self, hyperindividualism, as narcissism. And, of course, egoism and narcissism are often intimately connected.

Fromm (1980) offers a particularly interesting discussion of what he calls "group narcissism," the kind of thing found in people who assert, as many Americans do (or used to, at least) with such a sense of righteousness, "We're number one." We see this also in fans of sports teams. According to Fromm, group narcissism is tied to economic systems that are based on selfishness and attempts to maximize profits at the expense of others. That is, group narcissism is connected to the alienation one finds in modern industrial societies.

> The average person lives in social circumstances which restrict the development of intense narcissism. What should feed the narcissism of a poor man, who has little social prestige, whose children even tend to look down upon him? He is nothing—but if he can identify with his nation, then he is everything. (p. 50)

Group narcissism is very useful to governments when, for example, they want to mobilize people and get them ready to go to war. Fromm wonders whether modern men and women will die of narcissism because of their ego involvement in their hyper-technocratic industrial societies, just as Narcissus died because he fell in love with his own image in a pool of water.

Psychotherapists are increasingly interested in narcissism and are reportedly seeing narcissism in increasing numbers of patients. It is hard to say whether there is more narcissism now than in earlier times or whether therapists are simply more adept at recognizing it. Whatever the case, narcissism—in its many disguised forms—remains a problem of considerable significance, both for individuals and for American and other modern technological cultures.

Whether it is egoism or narcissism (or some combination of both) that is at fault, increasingly in U.S. culture the focus of our political energies has been on the individual and his or her rights, on private enterprise, and on personal ambitions, to the exclusion of the realm of the public and a sense of our collective responsibility and obligation. As a result, many critics suggest there is no equilibrium, and we have to find ways of dampening our narcissistic urges and inclinations and of directing our attention outward.

Sublimation

Sublimation, according to Freud, involves the rechanneling of sexual impulses from primary gratification by sexual intercourse into other forms or kinds of gratification that conform to the demands of society. The process of sublimation is unconscious and is a function of the ego, which, in a sense, "serves the id" and finds a way for sexual impulses to receive gratifications in socially approved ways. Freud (1963) describes the phenomenon of sublimation:

> We believe that civilization has been built up, under the pressure of the struggle for existence, by sacrifices in gratification of the primitive impulses, and that it is to a great extent forever being re-created, as each individual, successively joining the community, repeats the sacrifices of his instinctive pleasures for the common good. The

sexual are amongst the most important of the instinctive forces thus
utilized: they are in this way sublimated, that is to say, their energy
is turned aside from its sexual goal and diverted towards other
ends, no longer sexual and socially more valuable. But the structure thus built up is insecure, for the sexual impulses are with difficulty controlled. (p. 27)

Civilization, then, is based upon individuals' learning to control their sexual impulses (in part as the result of instruction and
coercion by social institutions) and finding other ways of gaining
gratification, such as in the arts, popular entertainments, and in
other endeavors. But because sexual impulses are powerful, there
is always a tension between them and the institutions developed
in societies. Civilization, as Freud points out in *Civilization and Its
Discontents* (1957), is the cause of many of our miseries: It forces
us to renounce uninhibited instinctual gratifications (and, in particular, genital satisfactions and aggressiveness), and it creates
guilt (channeling our aggressiveness back upon us): "The price of
progress in civilization is paid in forfeiting happiness through
the heightening of the sense of guilt" (p. 123).

Given all of this, the ability we have to sublimate our sexual
drives (and our aggressiveness must be included among them) and
to redirect our sexual energies into other areas where we receive
substitute gratifications is of immense importance. In recent
years the repressiveness of civilization has diminished, and people
are able (or seem to be able) to have much freer, less guilt-ridden
sexual relationships than in earlier times. Whether we can keep
the benefits of civilization and culture and maintain them in an
era of diminishing impulse control (both sexual and aggressive)
remains to be seen.

We now turn to discussion of a concept that explains why it is
so difficult, at times, to apply Freud's concepts to texts.

Overdetermination

Overdetermination refers to the fact that a given phenomenon (a
slip of the tongue, an image in a dream, or a symptom, for example)

can be the result of more than one factor, and may signify more than one thing. Freud uses the term in his discussion of dreams. He distinguishes, as noted above, between the manifest content of dreams, or what we can remember about them, and the latent content of dreams, or the dream thoughts—the wishes that motivate dreams and the images generated that constitute them. The latent dream is the images found in the dream and the manifest dream, by a process of secondary elaboration, turns these images, or tableaux, into a coherent (relatively speaking) narrative.

This situation is complicated because two different processes go on that confuse things—condensation and displacement. In condensation, as mentioned above, we construct collective, composite figures in which one thing can represent many different things (or, conversely, a number of different images can be combined into one). In displacement, as mentioned earlier, we substitute an element in a dream or image for other elements or images, generally replacing something overtly sexual with something whose sexuality is disguised.

> It thus seems plausible to suppose that in the dreamwork a psychical force is operating which on the one hand strips the elements which have a high psychical value of their intensity, and on the other hand, *by means of overdetermination,* creates from elements of low psychical value new values, which afterwards find their way into the dream-content. If that is so, a *transference and displacement of psychical intensities* occurs in the process of dream-formation, and it is as a result of these that difference between the text of the dream-content and that of the dream-thoughts comes about. (Freud, 1965, pp. 342-343)

Each detail in the manifest dream is tied to a number of details in the latent dream by the process of overdetermination. That is, there are generally multiple causes for a given element in a dream.

Another way to understand the phenomenon of overdetermination is to think of Saussure's division of the sign into a signifier and a signified. There can be many different signifiers that generate a particular signified. Or, more to the point, think of synecdoche, where a part can represent the whole or a whole can be represented by a part. Another analogy comes from medicine, where there are often a number of different physical problems that show themselves through one common symptom and several symptoms may be related to one problem.

Myth

A *myth*, in the context of this discussion, is a narrative that, among other functions, serves to connect individuals to their cultures and to explain natural and supernatural phenomena (including the creation of the world and the origins of humankind). Mark Shorer (1968), a distinguished literary critic, defines myth as follows: "Myths are the instruments by which we continually struggle to make our experience intelligible to ourselves. A myth is a large, controlling image that gives philosophical meaning to the facts of ordinary life" (p. 355).

There is usually a sacred dimension to our myths. Mircea Eliade (1961) distinguishes between the realms of the sacred and the profane, which he suggests are two different realms of being. The profane involves the world of science, of rationality, of empiricism. The sacred involves matters such as religious feeling, the irrational and unnatural aspects of life, a realm that is "numinous" (revealing the existence of divine power) and involves both time and space, which are existentially sacred. Eliade discusses the relation that exists between the sacred and myth as follows:

> The myth relates a sacred history, that is, a primordial event that took place at the beginning of time, *ab initio*. But to relate a sacred history is equivalent to revealing a mystery. For the persons of the myth are not human beings; they are gods or culture heroes and for this reason, their *gesta* constitutes mysteries; man could not know their acts if they were not revealed to him. The myth, then, is the history of what took place in *illo tempore*, the recitation of what the gods or the semi-divine beings did at the beginning of time. To tell a myth is to proclaim what happened *ab origine*. Once told, that is, revealed, the myth becomes apodictic truth; it establishes a truth that is absolute. (p. 95)

Myths, then, explain how things got started and function also as models for future action, because by describing the actions of the gods in the world, they imply that we should follow the gods' example. These myths, Eliade adds, become "the paradigmatic model for all human activities" (pp. 97-98).

The French anthropologist Claude Lévi-Strauss has dealt with myths in his work, and he suggests that we need to decode myths before we can understand what their "real" messages are. He argues that we must use structural analysis to understand (or deconstruct) myths and discover how they communicate and what their messages are. Myth is like language, he suggests, in that the meaning is not found in the isolated elements of the myth but in the way the elements are combined. These elements fall into bundles of relations, much as words become tied together in sentences. It is the bundles of these elements, what he calls relations, that are crucial and form the "true constituent units of a myth," not the elements themselves.

Lévi-Strauss describes his method of analyzing myths as follows. He breaks down a myth (he uses the term "story") into the shortest sentences he can and writes each sentence on a card, which is numbered and keyed to the story. Each card shows that a certain function is linked to a certain subject. He ends up with bundles of cards, each with a number on it that corresponds to some function in the story. Then he assembles the cards according to their functions: puts all the 1s together, all the 2s together, and so on. When he does this and assembles the cards that way, he is able to find the latent or hidden meaning of a myth.

Mary Douglas (1975), a British social anthropologist, discusses Lévi-Strauss's work:

> Briefly, its starting point is that it is the nature of the mind to work through form. Any experience is received in a structured form, and these forms or structures, which are a condition of knowing, are generally unconscious (as, for example, the unconscious categories of language). Furthermore, they vary little in modern or ancient times. They always consist of pairs of opposites, which are balanced against one another and built up in various (algebraically representable) ways. All the different kinds of patterned activity can be

analyzed according to the different structures they produce. . . . The
analysis of myth should proceed like the analysis of language. In
both language and myth the separate units have no meaning by
themselves, they acquire it only because of the way they are combined. (pp. 153-154)

This notion that myths are like language in generating meaning
by being tied to their opposites has echoes of Saussure's writings
on concepts having no meaning in themselves, but only by being
different from other concepts in their systems.

For Jungians, myths are direct expressions of the collective unconscious, and that explains why myths are found in similar forms
in all cultures and all ages and are, then, universal. The heroes of
myths, Jungians suggest, are archetypal—another reason they are
so similar in nature. For Freudians, the myth of Oedipus is of central importance in the human psyche and the core of all neurosis.
Many of the complexes discussed by Freudians (and some other
psychoanalytically inclined theorists) are tied, as we have seen,
to mythic heroes and heroines as well as to the heroes and
heroines of ancient dramatic works, who frequently have mythic
dimensions to them.

The study of myth and its relation to symbol and ritual continues to hold a central place in cultural studies, and has connections
to everything from psychological problems (Oedipus complex)
to political beliefs (the Marxist notion of the redeeming few).

Archetype

The concept of the archetype is associated most commonly with
Jungian theory. The term *archetype* refers to a universal image or
theme found in dreams, myths, religions, philosophies, and
works of art. Archetypes exist beyond the realm of the personal
unconscious of individuals; they are connected to past history
and an alleged collective unconscious found in all people. Archetypes, Jungians suggest, are unconscious. We become aware of
them only as the result of images in dreams and works of art or

of emotional experiences we have that connect us to them, suddenly, in ways that we do not immediately recognize. As Jung (1968) writes:

> What we properly call instincts are physiological urges, and are perceived by the senses. But at the same time, they also manifest themselves in fantasies and often reveal their presence only by symbolic images. These manifestations are what I call archetypes. They are without known origin; and they reproduce themselves in any time or in any part of the world—even where transmission by direct descent or "cross fertilization" through migration must be ruled out. (p. 58)

There are, Jung argues, symbolic expressions of natural phenomena that are not communicated from one person to another but are connected, somehow, to instinctual behavior or natural phenomena. As an example, Jung (1968) suggests that "the hero figure is an archetype, which has existed since time immemorial" (p. 61), and so is, he adds, the myth of Paradise or of a Golden Age, where people live in abundance and peace.

The existence of a collective unconscious, which is behind archetypes, is inferred. Jung goes on to suggest:

> We do not assume that each new-born animal creates its own instincts as an individual acquisition, and we must not suppose that human individuals invent their specific human ways with every new birth. Like the instincts, the collective thought patterns of the human mind are innate and are inherited. They function, when the occasion arises, in more or less the same way in all of us. (p. 64)

An analogy is drawn, then, between instincts in humans, which are natural and thus universal, and similar phenomena on the mental level. This would explain, Jungians argue, why myths are universal and certain themes or motifs are found in works of art all through history and all over the world. (Many critics, aestheticians, folklorists, and scholars from other disciplines disagree, I should point out.) Archetypes, Jungians suggest, inform our myths, religions, philosophies, and works of art, in addition to appearing in our dreams. Thus they play an important role in society.

The notion of the archetype (and of a collective unconscious that is connected to it) is very controversial, and many people reject it as being both unproven and unprovable. It may be possible to infer a collective unconscious that generates archetypes, but how does one demonstrate that it exists? (Some scholars have suggested that Jung's beliefs—especially the notions of the archetype and the mythical hero—are concepts that lent themselves to appropriation by the Nazis in Germany and supplied, indirectly, a rationale for fascism.) Jungian perspectives on heroes are considered in more detail in the next section.

Heroes

There are certain characteristics commonly associated with heroes in dramatic texts:

- They are good (in contrast to villains, who are evil).
- They are active (whereas many other characters are passive).
- They often find themselves rescuing damsels in distress and marrying them (or, in modern texts, having sex with them).
- They have extraordinary talents and skills (good with a gun, know martial arts, and the like).
- They win in the end (but not always).
- They often are modern manifestations of ancient mythical figures.
- They often have helpers, assistants, and tutelary figures to teach them important things.

According to Vladimir Propp (1928/1968), heroes have certain functions in narratives:

The hero of a fairy tale is that character who either directly suffers from the action of the villain in the complication (the one who senses some kind of lack), or who agrees to liquidate the misfortune or lack of another person. In the course of the action the hero is the person who is supplied with a magical agent (a magical helper), and who makes use of it or is served by it. (p. 50)

There are, Propp argues, two kinds of heroes: "victimized" heroes, who suffer at the hands of a villain and fight with and defeat the villain; and "seeker" heroes, who are "dispatched," sent on some mission and battle with villains as they try to accomplish their mission.

Although Propp did his work with a limited number of Russian folktales, his ideas have applicability to narratives in general, and many modern stories are, it can be argued, similar in nature to fairy tales (and may even be camouflaged versions of them, as far as their structure is concerned). (Propp's ideas are discussed in more detail in Chapter 4.)

Jungians are particularly interested in heroes and suggest that they are connected to our collective unconscious. As Joseph L. Henderson (1968) writes:

> The myth of the hero is the most common and the best known myth in the world. We find it in the classical mythology of Greece and Rome, in the Middle Ages, in the Far East, and among contemporary primitive tribes. It also appears in our dreams. . . .
>
> These hero myths vary enormously in detail, but the more closely one examines them the more one sees that structurally they are very similar. They have, that is to say, a universal pattern, even though they were developed by groups or individuals without any direct cultural contact with each other. . . . Over and over again one hears a tale describing a hero's miraculous but humble birth, his early proof of superhuman strength, his rapid rise to prominence or power, his triumphant struggle with the forces of evil, his fallibility to the sin of pride (*hybris*), and his fall through betrayal or heroic sacrifice that ends in his death. (p. 101)

The above deals with the tragic hero; ordinary heroes, especially those found in today's mass media, usually do not succumb to the sin of pride and survive, often to fight new villains in endless succession.

The basic function of the myth of the hero, Henderson adds, is to help individuals develop ego consciousness so they can deal with the problems they will confront as they live their lives. For Jungians, different heroes appear as human consciousness evolves. We need heroes, Henderson suggests, to help liberate us from regressive desires. Heroes, then, help people to separate and individuate themselves, which is why they have been with us all through history and why they are so important.

Shadow

In Jungian psychology, the shadow is the dark side of the psyche, which we tend to keep hidden from consciousness, an element in our personalities that must be recognized and dealt with. Henderson (1968) elaborates on the concept:

> Dr. Jung has pointed out that the shadow cast by the conscious mind on the individual contains the hidden, repressed and unfavorable (or nefarious) aspects of the personality. But this darkness is not just the simple converse of the conscious ego. Just as the ego contains unfavorable and destructive attitudes, so the shadow has good qualities—normal instincts and creative impulses. Ego and shadow, indeed, although separate, are inextricably linked together in much the same way that thought and feeling are related to one another. (p. 110)

Jung believes that there is a battle "for deliverance" between the shadow and the ego. Heroes provide the means by which, symbolically, the ego "liberates the mature man from a regressive longing to return to a blissful state of infancy in a world dominated by his mother" (Henderson, 1968, p. 110). This is symbolized in myths when a hero wins a battle against a dragon.

M.-L. von Franz (1968) adds, in her discussion of the process of individuation, that we can often see shadow aspects of other people that we refuse to recognize in ourselves. She offers, as examples, "egotism, mental laziness, and sloppiness; unreal fantasies, schemes, and plots; carelessness and cowardice; inordinate love of money and possessions" (p. 174). Manifestations of shadow also show up in impulsive and destructive acts by individuals and a susceptibility or tendency to be influenced by what von Franz calls collective "infections." We see the shadow, she adds, most easily in our dealings with people of the same sex, which is why, in our dreams, shadow figures are the same sex as the dreamer. Shadow figures are not one-dimensional but contain a number of different elements, and can include positive forces as well as negative aspects of our psyches.

This concept is not generally used in Freudian psychoanalytic criticism, but it is vaguely analogous to what Freud called the unconscious. The shadow, Jungians argue, is unconscious, but it has much more negativity to it than the Freudian unconscious. Jungians suggest that there is a kind of struggle for supremacy between the shadow and the ego, which reminds one of the struggle between the id and the ego in Freudian thought.

Both Freudians and Jungians would agree that where there are unconscious forces that are shaping behavior, there is likely to be trouble. It is better for ego elements in the psyche, defined broadly as rational and conscious decision making, to shape behavior, so that one can modify Freud's famous statement and say, "Where there is shadow or id, there should be ego."

Jungians and Freudians would disagree about the existence of archetypes that are passed down through history and are independent of the experiences of individuals. Freudians would interpret heroes and heroines in dreams in more personal terms than Jungians, who would see them as archetypal and connected more to general problems humans face than to particular problems individuals face.

We turn now to the final duality in Jungian thought—one that involves the relationship that exists between male and female elements in the human psyche.

Anima/Animus

The anima, in Jungian thought, represents the female element found in all males; the animus represents the male element found in all females.

In the Middle Ages, long before physiologists demonstrated that by reason of our glandular structure there are both male and female elements in all of us, it was said that "every man carries a woman within himself." It is this female element in every male that I have called the "anima." This "feminine" aspect is essentially a certain inferior kind of relatedness to the surroundings, and particularly to women, which is kept carefully concealed from others as well as from oneself. (Jung, 1968, pp. 14-15)

This duality is symbolized for Jungians in hermaphroditic figures, witches, priestesses, and the like in the arts and in tales, and in such occupations as medicine man and shaman, pursued in various archaic societies.

In the case of individuals in modern societies, Jungians hold that the anima is usually affected, if not shaped, by a man's mother. If the mother's influence is seen as negative, the anima aspects of the man's personality will be dark and have harmful effects. On the other hand, if the mother's influence is positive, the anima works to reinforce his sense of masculinity. Thus the anima can be either a positive or a negative force, leading to well-developed, integrated personalities or to disturbed ones.

M.-L. von Franz (1968) deals with the anima and animus and their impact on personality and their impact on the arts and related phenomena:

The most frequent manifestations of the anima takes the form of erotic fantasy. Men may be driven to nurse their fantasies by looking at films and strip-tease shows, or by day-dreaming over pornographic material. This is a crude, primitive aspect of the anima, which becomes compulsive only when a man does not sufficiently cultivate his feeling relationships—when his feeling attitude toward life has remained infantile. (p. 191)

On the positive side, however, von Franz suggests that it is the anima that enables us to find the right marriage partners and helps us explore inner values, leading to more profound insights into our psyches.

She suggests that there are four stages in the development of the animus, the male aspect of a woman's psyche:

1. the wholly physical man (e.g., Tarzan)
2. the romantic man (e.g., Shelley) or the man of action (e.g., Hemingway)
3. the bearer of the word (e.g., Lloyd George)
4. the wise guide to spiritual truth (e.g., Gandhi)

The animus functions in women the same way the anima does in men. The animus is formed, essentially, by a woman's father and can have good or bad influence. It can lead to coldness, obstinacy, and hypercritical behavior. In this negative aspect, it appears in myths and tales as the figure of Death or as a robber or death figure such as Bluebeard. On the positive side, it can help women gain inner strength, develop an enterprising approach to life, and achieve spiritual profundity. It also can teach them how to relate to men in more positive ways, as seen in many stories in which a woman's love redeems and saves men.

According to Jungians, the anima is an "inherited collective image of woman" that exists in man's unconscious, an archetype of past male-female relationships. The image a man has of women in general—and, in particular, the one he has of his mother—then is "projected" onto other women with whom the man has relationships. This can cause problems when the man does not realize he is projecting such an image onto women and thus does not see women as they really are. In like manner, women project their animus images onto men.

Conclusion

Our brief examination of psychoanalytic theory and cultural criticism is now complete. Between them, Freud and Jung wrote more than 40 books, and their followers have written hundreds, if not thousands more, so it has not been possible here to present more than a few of their most important ideas.

Freudian thought, more than Jungian thought, pervades the thinking of modern cultural critics and the general public as well, though we may not always recognize that this is the case. This invisibility, I would argue, is a result of its pervasiveness.

What is interesting about psychoanalytic thought, both Freudian and Jungian, is the degree to which the ideas associated with it can be used to analyze and interpret texts, works of art, and cultural phenomena of all kinds. Psychoanalytic theory enables us to interpret and understand texts in ways that other methods cannot, and explains things about texts to which other perspectives are, it would seem, blind. This is because psychoanalytic theory enables us, at least partly, to comprehend areas of our psyches that are emotional, intuitive, nonrational, hidden, repressed, suppressed, disguised—what you will. It is these areas that creative artists are somehow (probably intuitively) in touch with and most concerned with and that are, without psychoanalytic theory, not accessible to analysis or understanding.

I find that my students, as a rule, are extremely hostile to Freudian analysis, yet they are able to use Freud's ideas to analyze texts in considerable depth, and sometimes with a great deal of ingenuity. They find all kinds of applications of his concepts to the behavior of characters and the significance of symbols in texts. How is it, one may ask, that a methodology that is so "absurd" or "ridiculous" (terms they often use) can be applied to texts with such interesting results?

Auguste Comte

6

Sociological Theory
and Cultural Criticism

In this chapter I address sociological criticism—in the broadest sense of the term—and its application to cultural criticism. Sociology is a very large and amorphous field that covers an enormous number of areas. Within this field are scholars and writers with many different interests, philosophical positions, and methodological approaches. My focus here is on aspects of sociological thought that have relevance to cultural studies in general and to the media, popular culture, and related matters in particular.

I start with a discussion of a concept that is of central concern, culture. Although culture is the fundamental concept of anthropological thought, in its mass-mediated forms and with popular culture, specifically, it becomes a subject that is dealt with by sociologists as well as anthropologists and social scientists of all kinds, as well as literary theorists, critics, and analysts of varying persuasions.

Culture

Culture is one of the most dominant and elusive concepts used in contemporary discourse about society and the arts. This is because the concept is used by different people in different ways. For example, anthropologists see culture as the central organizing concept in their discipline. For them, *culture* refers to the pattern of beliefs and values, reflected in artifacts, objects, and institutions, that is passed on from generation to generation. It has been estimated that anthropologists have advanced more than a hundred definitions of culture. Let me offer a sampling of definitions here.

Culture is defined in the *Dictionary of Sociology and Related Terms* as follows:

> A collective name for all behavior patterns socially acquired and transmitted by means of symbols; hence a name for all the distinctive achievements of human groups, including not only such items as language, tool-making, industry, art, science, law, government, morals and religion, but also the material instruments or artifacts in which cultural achievements are embodied and by which intellectual cultural features are given practical effect, such as buildings, tools, machines, communication devices, art objects. . . . As culture is transmitted by processes of teaching and learning, whether formal or informal, by what is called "inter-learning," the essential part of culture is to be found in patterns embodied in the social traditions of the group, that is, the knowledge, ideas, beliefs, values, standards and sentiments prevalent in the group. (Fairchild, 1967, p. 80)

These groups, I should point out, vary considerably, depending upon all kinds of variables, such as region, religion, language, and socioeconomic class.

In his textbook *Cultural Anthropology*, Conrad Phillip Kottak (1987) offers a similar definition of culture. After pointing out that culture is distinctive to human beings who are members of society, he goes on:

> Culture encompasses rule-governed, shared, symbol-based, learned behavior and beliefs transmitted across the generations. Everyone is cultured, not just people with elite educations. The genus *Homo* has the capacity for Culture (in a general sense), but people live in specific cultures where they are raised according to different cultures. Culture rests on the human capacity for cultural learning, use of

language and symbols. *Culture* refers to customary beliefs and behavior and to the rules for conduct internalized in human beings through education. (p. 35)

The above definitions give us a good sense of how anthropologists interpret the term *culture* and point out that everyone has culture, though there are considerable differences in the cultures found in, for example, the United States and India, and in the subcultures found in each of those countries.

When the term *culture* is used in connection with the arts, it is often used to describe certain kinds of arts (so-called elite arts, which make up elite culture)—opera, ballet, "serious" poetry and novels, symphonic music, and other arts that require of audiences, generally speaking, elevated and educated tastes and refined sensibilities. People who go to symphonies, read classic novels, and attend the ballet, for example, are often described in popular parlance as "cultured." This would suggest, of course, that people who do not like these arts (but like what have been called the popular arts, the public arts, and mass culture) are "uncultured" or without culture, which is absurd.

There is, then, another kind of culture, which we call *popular culture*, a term generally used to describe such things as comic strips, most television programs and radio shows, formulaic novels (such as romances, detective novels, and science fiction novels), popular music (rock, rap, country-western, and so on), fashions, fads, and sports. That is, popular culture is made up of massmediated culture and other related aspects of culture that are generally consumed by large numbers of people on a continual basis.

Sometimes it is difficult to say where works of popular art stop being popular and become elite, or vice versa. If Shakespeare's *Hamlet* is broadcast on television, does it become popular culture? Many critics and cultural theorists argue that except at the extremes (perhaps with avant-garde string quartets on one end of a continuum and professional wrestling at the other end), elite and popular culture are very similar, overlap to considerable degrees, or, for all practical purposes, are the same. (This argument, let us recall, is also made by postmodernists.)

TABLE 6.1 Perceived Differences Between Popular Culture
                    and Elite Culture

Popular Culture	Elite Culture
romance novels	classic novels
rock music	symphonies, string quartets
musical comedy	opera
situation comedy	classical comedy
(e.g., *Seinfeld, Roseanne*)	(e.g., *Twelfth Night, Volpone*)
comic strips	paintings

Even people who like the elite arts may also have a taste for popular culture. Many people who might go to the symphony on Friday night would also enjoy a football game on Saturday afternoon, or who read "serious" novels during the day like to watch situation comedies, action-adventure shows, or the like at night. Table 6.1 lists some of the commonly held differences between elite and popular cultures.

I will pursue this topic in more detail in the discussion of popular culture, but several points should be made in passing. First, as noted above, at the extremes it is easy to see that the differences between popular culture and elite culture can be considerable, but in the middle, it can be hard to discern any differences (e.g., what about pop art, jazz, and comic books that evolve into graphic novels?). Second, it does not make sense to discuss popular culture and elite culture essentially in terms of their aesthetic qualities and neglect their audiences and their social and cultural impacts, which is commonly done, especially in work dealing with the elite arts.

The study of popular culture has merged with the study of elite culture to lead to a new metadiscipline, cultural studies. Now we find sociologists, anthropologists, political scientists, philosophers, English and humanities professors, and people in American studies (and in recent years, now that it has emerged as a discipline of its own, communication scholars) studying whatever aspects of culture, high or low, popular or unpopular, they find interesting. Everyone (as the late Jimmy Durante put it) wants to get into the act. From the perspective of cultural studies, all culture is worth analyzing and interpreting, and the distinctions that used to be made between elite arts and popular arts are no longer held as useful or valid, for reasons that will be explained below.

Multiculturalism

Cultural critics believe that culture plays an important role in social and political developments as well as in the development of individual identity. We now see identity in two ways: There is personal identity, which involves what is distinctive about a given individual (appearance, intelligence, personality), and social identity, which involves the numerous groups a person belongs to—sexual, economic, racial, ethnic, religious, political, and so on.

The focus of multiculturalism, as it applies to the books students read and the texts they consider (films, dramas, music, and so on) in English courses and humanities and history courses (and others as well), is on the adequate representation of minority cultures in the literary and cultural canon. Minority cultures generally have been either excluded or ignored, as a result of which, it is asserted, students are exposed only to narrow and distorted perspectives on U.S. culture and society. And those in the excluded groups get distorted images of themselves. Thus the traditional world history courses or introduction to humanities courses, critics argue, have focused on dead white European males (or DWEMs—pronounced "dweems") and have neglected works by women, African Americans, Asian Americans, Latinos, gays, and others.

The argument made by those advocating multiculturalism is that because the United States is a multicultural society, with large numbers of women, Latinos, Asian Americans, African Americans, Native Americans, and so on, works by these people should be included in the literary and philosophical canon (the novels and plays and philosophy books assigned by professors and read by students). Instead of a focus on DWEMs and WASPs (white Anglo-Saxon Protestants), and on topics such as national character and consensus in U.S. history (what might be called a dominant unicultural perspective), for example, the focus should be on diversity and the contributions of various minority groups to American life. This material should be added to the canon for two primary reasons: First, such a change would recognize the contributions of the various cultures to literary, philosophical, and other areas; and second, it would help students who are members of minority groups to attain stronger senses of identity, both personal and social. The unicultural perspective is, to use the language of some of the groups who claim to be underrepresented, Eurocentric and phallocentric (and perhaps logocentric), among other things.

The old idea of assimilating into a dominant WASP American culture and casting off, to the extent possible, one's ethnic or minority identity has been replaced by an emphasis on maintaining minority or subcultural identities and, at the same time, being American. The melting pot metaphor of cultural homogenization has been replaced by the beef stew metaphor, in which the essential elements in the stew maintain their discrete identities yet are part of something that includes, and is flavored by, all.

The movement toward multiculturalism in the United States is particularly significant because in many cities and states whites are no longer in the majority; instead, they make up the largest minority. Even so, advocates of multicultural education assert, whites control the educational system and thus are able to impose (either through conscious design or unwittingly) their perspective on things and their choices as far as what novels, stories, plays, and works of social thought and philosophy are read by students.

There are a number of problems involved with the desire to redefine the curriculum in multicultural terms. Let's take the example of philosophy. First, are there works of philosophy by representatives of the various minority cultures that are as important as the works of such so-called DWEM philosophers as Plato, Aristotle, Spinoza, Kant, Hume, and Locke? (Note that, aside from Hume and Locke, the others in this list could legitimately be described as ethnics.) If we decide that it is necessary to insert works by minority groups into the curriculum, should inferior works be selected for their alleged "sociological" (group identity-enhancing) benefits? It may be, of course, that we have neglected great works because we are so fixated on our DWEMs, in which case a good argument can be made for expanding the canon.

Second, if there are great works to be found in the literature of various multicultural groups, how do we choose which ones to take? There are so many different groups that not all can be represented. How do we decide which books to add to the canon? Finally, will the focus on multiculturalism eventually destroy the sense of unity that has traditionally been part of American life (even though there has been a great deal of conflict in American society)? Will multiculturalism lead to anarchy and chaos, as group identities overwhelm national identity? Or will it lead to a more realistic understanding of American culture and society?

DWEMs

As suggested above, some proponents of multiculturalism and some feminists talk about the content of most courses on Western history or world history or literature (and related courses) as being confined, in large measure, to the ideas and works of DWEMs— dead white European males. The argument is that the ideas and works of women and people of color have been neglected and the ideas and works of DWEMs have been overemphasized.

This critique of the way history and cultural studies are taught has led in a number of directions. Some African American scholars argue that the origins of so-called Western civilization are in Africa, and that many of the ideas (and even a number of the philosophers and writers) that we think of as originating among whites in fact came from blacks. (These views, I should add, are not accepted by most scholars.) Some feminist cultural critics argue that our culture is phallocentric, and that the contributions of women thinkers, artists, poets, writers, and so on have been underemphasized and underappreciated. Those who create the philosophical and literary canon—the list of works considered to be classics and that tend to be found in courses dealing with civilization and culture—argue that when an Asian or African thinker creates works as significant as those of Kant or Hegel or Marx in philosophy or Cervantes or Dostoyevsky or Proust in literature, they will be added to the canon.

In recent years, many universities and colleges have broadened their civilization courses and added works by thinkers and creative artists who are not DWEMs, so students can be exposed to a broader understanding of the nature of social, political, and philosophical thought and creative activity and to the contributions of women and people of color to the world's intellectual and artistic heritage.

Currently, the fields of contemporary literary theory and communication and cultural studies are dominated by the work of LWEMs (living, or recently deceased, white European males) such as Jacques Derrida, Ferdinand de Saussure, Sigmund Freud, Roman Jakobson, Tzvetan Todorov, Paul de Man, Claude Lévi-Strauss, Roland Barthes, Michel Foucault, Umberto Eco, Yuri Lotman (of the Tartu school of semiotics), and Mikhail Bakhtin. There are relatively few American, South American, Asian, or African scholars, male or female, whose work is internationally significant in these fields. American scholars, male and female, have tended, in the past at least, to work in more empirical fields, and have done less philosophical and speculative work. Our cultural critics generally adapt and apply the theories of European thinkers such as those mentioned above.

The assertion that our colleges and universities are focusing too much attention on the work of dead white European males is connected to another issue, the matter of political correctness, which includes how members of minorities and other groups are to be addressed.

Political Correctness

Political correctness is a term whose definition is currently under contention. Conservatives use it to castigate professors on the political left (especially Marxists) who they allege have poli-

ticized English and humanities courses with left-wing and Marxist ideologies. These leftist scholars, it is claimed, use political
correctness to attack scholars with opposing views and to impose
a rigid antiestablishment perspective, a left-wing orthodoxy, on
literary studies and related concerns. They are joined in this, it is
asserted, by representatives of many minority groups—ethnic,
racial, sexual, and so on—who, among other concerns, wish to be
identified in certain ways (though in some cases there are disputes within the groups themselves about what they should be
called).

Leftist and other scholars argue that *political correctness* is a term
used by conservatives to discredit divergent (that is, radical, socialist, leftist, Marxist, feminist, and other) perspectives on politics
and culture, and that conservatives wish to impose an essentially
right-wing orthodoxy in the academy. Political correctness is tied
up with the matter of multiculturalism: Conservatives tend to
oppose implementing courses with multicultural perspectives
and liberals (and others on the left) stress the importance of such
courses.

The issue of political correctness includes a great deal of attention to language and how various groups are identified by others,
in the press and in everyday conversation. This stems from the
belief that, as linguists have explained, the language that we use
to describe others, whether groups or individuals, affects the way
we think about them. Disputes over language have resulted in
the institution of speech codes on some campuses in attempts to
protect members of various racial, ethnic, religious, and other
groups from verbal abuse. Do individuals on campuses have a
First Amendment right to attack verbally or insult individuals
based on those individuals' membership in particular groups?
Or, in doing so, do those who use insulting and abusive language
deny those they direct their language against of their rights?

As a result of the focus on the rights of minority groups, many
traditional practices are being attacked, practices that in the past
most people never gave much thought to. For example, Native
Americans are asking sports teams, colleges, and other organizations that use images or symbols of Native Americans in their

logos, seals, or names (a celebrated case being the Washington Redskins) to change their names or eliminate the images, because they see these practices as demeaning and insulting. As a society, we face a dilemma. At what point, we must ask, are members of these various groups being too "picky" or unreasonable? How far do we go to deal with their needs and rights? This matter is currently being worked out in various areas.

In truth, the matter of political correctness seems to have been blown out of proportion; it has never become an issue at most universities. Only a relatively small number of institutions of higher learning have had major campuswide controversies concerning subjects related to political correctness. Some adherents of political liberalism (and a multicultural perspective) argue that the furor over political correctness was created by conservatives who needed an enemy to frighten Americans with when they lost the old threat of communism. They assert that because Americans no longer have communists to worry about, the conservatives have set up multiculturalists to take their place. Some adherents of political conservatism argue that students are being brainwashed by left-wing professors and that the right to free speech is being attacked. What has happened, actually, is that the political correctness issue—to a great degree a tempest in a teapot—has subsided in most institutions. But it did raise an important issue: At what point is the consensus needed to maintain an institution, and society in general, at risk of being destroyed? What happens when people no longer accept the norms, the rules, the values that are dominant in a society? It is to that subject we now turn.

Anomie

Anomie, a term coined by the French sociologist Émile Durkheim (1951), means "no norms." It is derived from the Greek word *nomos,* or norm. Anomic individuals and groups do not subscribe, generally speaking, to the norms, laws, or rules of society at large. Thus, for example, a band of thieves may be made up of individuals who are not alienated but anomic. The same would apply to what were once called deviant subcultures, such as the gay community. Members of subcultures do follow certain codes of behavior, but often these codes are at variance with the codes found in the larger society. Some sociologists have suggested that deviance is related to, and perhaps even generated by, anomie.

Durkheim distinguishes between "mechanical" and "organic" solidarity. Mechanical solidarity is found in primitive societies and, today, in the family, where one has a sense of belonging. Organic solidarity, on the other hand, is found in modern societies and is characterized not by a feeling of belonging to something but, instead, by a complex system of contractual or legalistic relationships. According to Durkheim, we have moved from social arrangements that were essentially mechanical to ones that are essentially organic, and, although this represents progress, in a sense it also has its costs.

One of these costs is anomie. In societies characterized by mechanical solidarity, social relations become fragmented and transitory and people lose sight of a collective consciousness where common meanings are elaborated, of a commonly accepted sense of what is right and wrong, good and bad. This paves the way for individuals or subcultures to create their own rules and for anomic behavior. In the United States and many other Western countries, we often find anomic behavior in adolescents, who are (for various reasons) rebellious, and in old people, who, because of our social arrangements, find themselves left out of things. They feel lonely and isolated.

Anomie, it should be pointed out, is a social phenomenon that affects individuals. It is the consequence not of specific individuals' being unable to fit into their societies, but of the structure of societies and the arrangements these societies make for adolescents, old people, and members of other subcultures, "deviant" groups, and so on. These societies could be described, as far as their ability to integrate certain kinds of individuals into them, as not functioning very well. This leads to our next topic, one of the most fundamental in social and political thought: functionalism.

Functionalism

Functionalism (also known as structural-functionalism) is a theory, held by some sociologists and anthropologists, that sees society as a system and stresses the roles that various institutions, entities, and practices play in the maintenance of this system. Something is functional if it helps maintain the system, dysfunctional if it leads to the breakdown of the system, and nonfunctional if it plays no role in the system in which it is involved. In addition, sociologists often make a distinction, elaborated by Robert Merton (1957), between manifest functions, which are planned, obvious, and intended, and latent functions, which are accidental and unintended, and of which we are generally unaware.

Some social scientists hold that it is the latent or unintended consequences of practices and institutions that are of major concern, for they keep institutions functioning and, in effect, help maintain society. Once we discover these latent functions and point them out, they can no longer work as they did, so this kind of sociological knowledge ultimately, ironically, helps destabilize society.

Sociologists who use functional analysis investigate various practices and institutions and seek to discover their latent functions, thereby making these functions manifest. Other sociologists and social scientists have elaborated lists of "functional prerequisites," found in all social systems—lists that are often so abstract or general that they have had negligible utility.

Functionalism has been attacked by critics who argue that it tends to neglect conflict and power and is essentially static—more concerned with what maintains the status quo and sustains equilibrium in societies than with phenomena that do not play these roles and lead to change in or, in some cases, the breakdown of the system.

Michael Thompson, Richard Ellis, and Aaron Wildavsky (1990) have modified traditional functional analysis; they suggest a method that they call "cultural-functional analysis." They argue that traditional functional analysis in the social sciences has been flawed in the way it has been executed, but it is not inherently flawed, and they assert that the adoption of cultural-functional analysis enables social scientists to avoid many of the errors made by earlier functionalists. They point out that functionalism has been criticized for being ideologically conservative:

> Another charge commonly leveled against functionalist explanation is that it commits one to an ideologically conservative perspective— that by showing a behavior's purpose one is therefore predisposed against changing it. Though past functionalists may have often pursued a conservative agenda, our contention is that functionalist explanation per se is ideologically neutral. . . . Cultural-functional analysis pursues what we believe is a more fruitful task of asking how types of social relations vary and how these different modes of social relations vary in the resources they can employ to resolve internal conflicts. (p. 107)

Rather than looking for functional requisites that allegedly exist in all societies, cultural-functionalists look at how different forms of social relations are established and how they function.

Following Merton's lead, these theorists move functionalist analysis down from a rather abstract "societal" level and use it to analyze different groups with varying values, beliefs, ways of life, and so on. They posit a situation in which various groups are continually changing and continually in conflict, so that what is functional for one group—and, in particular, one political culture— is dysfunctional for another group or political culture. Thompson et al. conclude that the great sociologists all used functional analysis because they needed it to explain how societies hold together. For cultural critics, functionalism is also an important concept, for it is the functions of texts and the mass media that Marxist and sociological critics deal with in their work on media effects (including their social and political consequences).

Consider, for example, the functions of religious institutions. They help, as a rule, to keep a society together by providing certain values and beliefs that their followers hold. However, in cases where two antagonistic religions exist, religious institutions can be the source of terrible conflict; thus, in certain situations, religious institutions are destabilizing and dysfunctional. We also must consider the latent functions of religions, for much of what individuals do, even those who may think they are not affected by religion, is tied to religious teachings and the realm of what sociologists call "the sacred."

Sacred/Profane

Durkheim spells out the distinction between the sacred and the profane in *The Elementary Forms of the Religious Life* (1967). In this book, a classic study of religious thought and its relation to the social order, Durkheim explains how religious thought divided the world into two distinct spheres:

> All known religious beliefs, whether simple or complex, present one common characteristic: they presuppose a classification of all things, real and ideal, of which men think, into two classes or opposed groups, generally designated by two distinct terms which are translated well enough by the words *profane* and *sacred* (profane, sacre). (p. 52)

This notion that there are two diametrically opposed realms brings us back to the work of Ferdinand de Saussure (1966), who argues that concepts have no meanings in themselves but derive their meanings from being in systems or networks of relationships. Their meanings are differential, and not defined by positive content but negatively, by their relationships with other concepts. Thus the sacred cannot exist without the profane, and vice versa. Durkheim continues:

> This division of the world into two domains, one containing all that is sacred, the other all that is profane, is the distinctive trait of religious thought; the beliefs, myths, dogmas and legends are either representations or systems of representations which express the nature of sacred things, the virtues and powers which are attributed to them, or their relations with each other and with profane things. (p. 52)

This concept, he adds, extends beyond the realm of gods to all kinds of things—a tree, a rock, a house, anything, in fact, can be sacred if people feel that it is sacred and think of it as sacred.

Mircea Eliade (1961), whose ideas are discussed in Chapter 5, elaborates upon this distinction. He explains that space and time can be sacred, defines myths as relating a sacred history, and, of particular interest to culture analysts, suggests that many of the things that contemporary people do are really camouflaged versions of ancient sacred rites. As he puts it, "The modern man who feels and claims that he is nonreligious still retains a large stock of camouflaged myths and degenerated rituals" (pp. 204-205). Let me list and summarize some of the points Eliade makes:

1. Such events as New Year's parties, moving into a new house, and celebrations of promotions all exhibit, in laicized form, the ancient rituals of renewal.

2. The cinema deals with ancient motifs, such as battles between heroes and monsters, initiation ordeals and combats, and the experience of paradise and hell.

3. Utopian movements such as Marxism are tied to the eschatological myth of the redeeming few.

4. Nudism and sexual freedom movements are connected to the notion of human innocence before the Fall and a nostalgia for Eden.

5. Psychoanalysis is a modernized version of ancient initiation ordeals and battles with monsters.

In short, Eliade argues, most people, even those who feel they are nonreligious, still believe in pseudoreligious and degenerated mythologies. This is to be expected, he explains, because "profane man is the descendent of *homo religiosus* and he cannot wipe out his own history—that is, the behavior of his religious ancestors which had made him what he is today" (p. 209).

The related concepts of the sacred and the profane are useful to analysts of culture because they provide insight that helps explain much contemporary behavior. Much of what we do, without our recognizing it, has a sacred and therefore religious dimension. It has even been suggested by some theorists, such as George

Gerbner, that television and the mass media in general have a religious or sacred dimension. This leads us to our next subject, the mass media.

Mass Media Theory

Over the years, those scholars who have studied and done research with the mass media (sociologists, psychologists, social psychologists, anthropologists, literary scholars, and now people who get advanced degrees in communication itself) have developed a number of theories that deal with the roles of the media in society, their impacts, and related concerns. The theories fall into two general camps: those that argue that the media are powerful and those that say the media have minimal impact on individuals and societies. Marxist media theorists are found in the first camp; they suggest that the media spread bourgeois ideology and play an important role in maintaining the capitalist system. "Hypodermic" theorists, who argue that all members of an audience get the same message, are also in this camp. Uses and gratifications theorists, who give individuals a significant role in the interpretation of texts, are found in the second camp, as are many other kinds of theorists. They see the media as, perhaps, reinforcing beliefs and values, but not as profoundly shaping them.

Much of the research conducted so far on the mass media has been of a social psychological nature, focusing on such matters as opinion formation and attitude change. This research has generally been quantitative, generating data that can be "massaged," and has thus been seen as "scientific." In recent years, however, theorists influenced by Marxism, semiotics, and Continental philosophy have become interested in texts and the way they generate meaning, leading to major changes in the ways researchers approach the mass media. Studies of the mass media and popular culture have now become part of cultural studies.

Some of the most important theories of the mass media are described briefly below:

Uses and gratifications theory: Here the emphasis moves from the effects of mass media on people to the ways people use mass media and the various gratifications they get from the media. This theory suggests that media users are active rather than passive and are selective in their choices of media experiences.

Dependency theory: This theory deals with the way people rely on the mass media for information and the dependencies on the media that people develop especially when there is a great deal of social change occurring and people have a high level of anxiety.

Agenda-setting theory: According to this theory, the media tend to focus on certain issues and neglect others, and thus function so as to set the agenda and shape what people will consider in making social and political decisions. The media, according to this theory, do not tell people what to think but, rather, what to think *about*—in so doing, they shape the agendas for people and societies.

Cultivation theory: The focus in this theory, developed by George Gerbner (1977), is on the relationship that exists between the mass media's presentation of reality (and television's in particular) and what audiences perceive to be reality. Because the media, and television is the most important of the media, present a distorted view of reality—for instance, in terms of how much crime there is and how dangerous life is—heavy consumers of the media and viewers of television gain unrealistic pictures of reality.

Gatekeeping theory: This theory is concerned with the individuals in media organizations who "guard the gates," those who determine, in the case of news, for example, which stories will be covered and which will be neglected. Editors and others in media organizations decide what stories are important and what audiences want to know (and maybe, in some cases, need to know), and thus filter out some stories and let other stories be published or broadcast.

Two-step flow theory: This theory argues that there are individuals, opinion leaders, who play a role in the way media affect societies. The media do not have direct impacts on individuals, according to this theory; the impacts occur through two steps. The first step is media influence on opinion leaders, who may be (but are not always) members of the society's socioeconomic elite. The second step takes place when these opinion leaders, in their interpersonal relationships, influence how the other people with whom they interact perceive the media. Thus opinion leaders function somewhat like gatekeepers, but in society at large rather than in media organizations.

Hypodermic theory: This theory, no longer accepted by most communication researchers, suggests that mass media texts are very powerful, and that their messages are more or less irresistible; the media are seen to behave like a hypodermic needle, injecting audiences with their messages. We now have evidence to suggest that audiences are selective in their choices of media to consume, that individuals interpret given texts in a variety of different ways, and, according to reception theorists, even play a role in creating texts.

Spiral of silence theory: According to this theory, elaborated by German public opinion theorist Elisabeth Noelle-Neumann (1974), people who hold views that they believe are not popular or widely held tend to keep quiet. At the same time, those who perceive their views to be accepted state them ever more strongly, leading to a spiral in which certain views tend to be suppressed and other views gain prominence. Thus the views of minorities tend to be seen as weaker than they actually are and the views of majorities are perceived as stronger than they really are.

Mass Society

The *mass* in mass society theories refers not so much to large numbers of people as to their alleged separation from one another and feelings of isolation and estrangement (there are large societies, such as found in India and China, where traditional ways of behavior link people together in coherent units). Another element of a mass society is the existence of highly routinized, bureaucratic institutions, where individuals experience a loss of a sense of personal identity. A good metaphor for a mass society is a beach, where the grains of sand are all in the same place, but separate from one another.

Mass society theory, developed by social theorists at the end of the 19th century, tied the changes from traditional to modern society to the development of a mass society. Marx had argued that the development of capitalism leads to alienation and the radical estrangement of individuals from themselves and from others. Ferdinand Tönnies (1887/1957) elaborated a theory in which he asserted that societies had moved from gemeinschaft (relations based on trust and close ties, such as those found in the family and small communities) to gesellschaft (relations based on contracts and legalistic ties, such as one finds in the corporation).

Thus modernization and urbanization were, social theorists argued, leading to a mass society characterized by the development of classes and social differentiation, by anomie (and confusion about mores and proper ways of behaving), by increasing conflict, and by lack of communication among members of society. As Shearon Lowery and Melvin L. DeFleur (1983) point out:

> The concept of mass society is significant for the study of media for two reasons. First, in spite of the fact that the theoretical picture it provides of contemporary society is overdrawn, we can recognize at least some of these trends around us. We *have* undergone industrialization, urbanization, modernization. Life in contemporary society is very different because of these changes than it was in the "good old days" of traditional society. . . .
> But more important, it was this conceptualization of mass society that dominated the thinking of those intellectuals who were first concerned about the effects of the new mass media. (p. 11)

It was assumed that people who lived in a mass society, separated from one another and without groups to give them identity, would be easily manipulated by the mass media, as the "magic bullet" theory of the media suggests. This manipulation would eventuate in some kind of a totalitarian society.

In 1895, Gustav Le Bon, a French social theorist, wrote *The Crowd*, a classic work that deals with the concept of the crowd and the influence of crowds on history. He offers a rationale for believing in the "magic bullet" theory in his discussion of theatrical representations:

> Nothing has greater effect on the imagination of crowds than theatrical representations. The entire audience experiences at the same time the same emotions, and if these emotions are not at once transformed into acts, it is because the most unconscious spectator cannot ignore that he is the victim of illusions, and that he has laughed or wept over imaginary adventures. Sometimes, however, the sentiments suggested by the images are so strong that they tend, like habitual suggestions, to transform themselves into acts. (Le Bon, 1895/1960, p. 68)

The notion that an entire audience experiences the same emotions—that is, gets the same thing out of a theatrical representation or, in current terms, the mass media—is at the heart of the magic bullet theory.

The notion of the mass society is not in vogue anymore. Tocqueville (1956) pointed out long ago that Americans tend to belong to many voluntary associations, and that would suggest that we are not (and have never been) as isolated and alienated as mass society theorists would suggest. These voluntary associations would also, so the theory goes, prevent the rise of extremism, because members would be pulled in different directions and would not become single-issue fanatics. Furthermore, reception theorists now argue that individuals tend to decode texts in highly personal ways, rather than all getting one message. The belief that mass-mediated texts can have uniform effects on atomized masses has not been supported by research, either.

It is best, then, to see the concept of the mass society from a historical point of view. It was connected to the ideas of a number of social theorists who were trying to make sense of the changes taking place at the end of the 19th century. Their ideas did have an element of truth, but ultimately they were too simplistic and reductionist to do justice to the societies that have developed in the 20th century. In fact, it could be argued now that some of the problems we face in contemporary societies stem from the fact that people have allegiances to groups (ethnic, religious, nationalistic, philosophical) that are so strong that in some cases they distort the individuals' perceptions of reality and create trouble for the democratic process.

Media/Medium

A medium, in communications parlance, is something that facilitates the transmission of something (words, images, sounds) from one source, typically a "sender," to another source, typically a "receiver." The most important mass media, in terms of their popularity and impacts, are television, radio, film, records, newspapers, magazines, and books. The general category labels attached to these media are *photoelectronic* and *print*.

There is a considerable amount of disagreement among scholars about the role of media: What impact does a medium have on the "message" it is carrying, and what impact do the media, in general, have on the societies in which they are found? Marshall McLuhan, a celebrated and controversial media theorist, distinguishes between print media, which are linear and thus encourage rationality, and electronic media, which surround us ("all-at-onceness" rather than linearity) and thus, according to McLuhan, encourage emotional responses to messages. Print, he suggests, leads to uniformity, continuity, individualism, and nationalism. Electronic media lead us in the opposite directions.

McLuhan has assigned the medium more importance than the messages it carries, stating that "the medium is the message," which is the title of the first chapter of his book *Understanding Media: The Extensions of Man* (1965). In this book, he also makes a controversial distinction between "hot" media and "cold" media (see Table 6.2). Oppositions can help us to see relationships more clearly, and we should think of hot and cool in terms of paired opposites or related topics.

McLuhan argues that the medium is more important than the message it carries because "the effects of technology do not occur at the level of opinions or concepts, but alter sense ratios or patterns of perception steadily and without resistance" (p. 18). It is more

TABLE 6.2 Examples of Hot Media and Cold Media

Hot Media	Cold Media
high definition (full of data)	low definition (few data)
low participation (excludes)	high participation (includes)
radio	telephone
movie	television show
photograph	cartoon
printed word	speech
phonetic alphabet	hieroglyphics, ideograms
lecture	seminar
book	dialogue
city slicker	rustic
modern civilization	tribes
city	town
nylon stockings	open mesh stockings

SOURCE: Based on McLuhan (1965, chap. 2).

important, he suggests, to shape the way we perceive the world than to give us ideas or shape our opinions. In recent years, McLuhan's work has fallen into disfavor and neglect—in part because his style of writing (slick and gimmicky) offends many people and in part because his theories about media are thought to be somewhat simplistic. They are very suggestive, however, and may have been dismissed too quickly.

At one time, some media theorists held that the media merely "transport" sounds, images, messages, and so on, and that the media themselves play no significant role in the content of the material transmitted. This theory is now being debated. Tony Schwartz (1974), a media theorist and prominent maker of advertisements, has argued that the function of the media is not to carry information so much as it is to hit a responsive chord in audiences:

> The critical task is to design our package of stimuli so that it resonates with information already stored with the individual and thereby induces the desired learning or behavioral effect. Resonance takes place when the stimuli put into our communication evoke *meaning* in a listener or viewer. That which we put into the communication has no meaning in itself. The meaning of our

communication is what a listener or viewer *gets out* of his experience with the communicator's stimulus. (pp. 24-25)

Thus the media function most effectively when they stimulate
people and activate material already stored in the minds of audiences and generate desired responses. Much of that stored material, it should be pointed out, was put in the heads of the audiences by the media in the first place. Schwartz's emphasis on the
term *meaning* also suggests the importance of semiotic analysis,
which is one of the primary ways of determining how people
find meaning in sounds and images.

Studying the media and the texts the media transmit has become an important topic, as the media, and particularly television, are playing an ever increasing role in our lives. The average
person in the United States watches close to four hours of television each day, and also listens to the radio a considerable amount,
reads newspapers and magazines, and, occasionally, reads books.

Much of what cultural critics study is mass-mediated, though
literary scholars tend to place more emphasis on the texts carried
(novels, poems, and so on) than on the media carrying the texts
(print). There is also a growing interest in media aesthetics, and
now courses on visual literacy and related matters are found in
our universities, especially in schools of journalism and mass
communication. Political scientists also study the mass media,
because they play an important role in our elections and in shaping
our consciousness.

Audience

An audience, for our purposes, can be thought of as a number
of people who are exposed to a particular text. They can be in the
same place (as in a theater or at a football game) or widely scattered,
in their own homes, as in the case of audiences for radio programs and television programs.

Mass media outlets in the United States are businesses that
make money by selling print advertising and radio and television

commercials. This means that the basic commercial function of the media is to deliver audiences to advertisers. (In this sense, the programs carried by television, for example, can be seen as filler between the commercials. The programs are created to attract certain kinds of audiences for the commercials.) The demographic and psychographic makeup of these audiences is of paramount importance to advertisers. Sellers of upscale products want to reach audiences made up of people who can afford these products and may be motivated to purchase them.

Advertising agencies and market research companies have been very creative in devising ways of characterizing audiences. For example, SRI (formerly Stanford Research Institute) has elaborated a typology based on values and lifestyles of audiences, and this is but one of many different typologies or classification schemes.

In terms of media and cultural analysis, there are a number of other considerations to keep in mind relative to audiences. I dealt with these earlier, but I want to call them to your attention once again:

1. artists, writers, and so on who create the texts
2. artworks (texts), such as books, films, television shows, and songs
3. America (society) and its value systems, beliefs, and so on
4. audiences who watch television shows, go to films, listen to radio, go to concerts, and so on (i.e., those who receive the texts)
5. media, which make the texts available to audiences

The audience, then, is but one element of the system of mass media. But because of the nature of the mass media in the United States, where media outlets are primarily businesses that exist to make a profit, things are skewed. It can be argued that audiences (or, more precisely, the perceptions of audiences held by those who own the media and those who create the texts spread by media) exercise hegemony over the process.

That is why so much of the material in the mass media is of such poor quality. "We're just giving the people what they want," argue those who run the media. Whether the audiences get what they like or learn to like what they get is a question that is continually being debated. Advances in new technologies may play a role here, for soon people will be able to access, from their homes, hundreds and maybe even thousands of cable channels or channels beamed down from satellites. Whether these channels will enhance our choices or give us more of the same is another matter.

Stereotyping

A stereotype is a group-shared image of some category of people, a greatly oversimplified notion or belief about what individuals who are members of some group (racial, gender, ethnic, religious, occupational, or whatever) are like. From a logical standpoint, stereotypes are based on a fallacious premise:

All X are Y.
John (or Jane) is an X.
Therefore, John (or Jane) is a Y.

The X here can be African Americans, WASPs, Jews, southerners, Mexicans, gays or lesbians, various so-called deviant groups, those who have certain occupations, Republicans, Italians, Scots, and so on. The Y is some attribute that large numbers of people believe is characteristic of the particular group. Thus we have stereotypes of African Americans as criminals, WASPs as cold and unemotional, Jews as materialistic, southerners as racist rednecks, Mexicans as lazy, lawyers as unscrupulous, Republicans as country-club fat cats, Italians as dirty or involved in organized crime, and Scots as being cheap (or "thrifty," a more positive term).

It is the generalization to all members of a group that makes stereotypes problematic. Some people in a group may tend to have certain characteristics, but this does not mean that one can ascribe those characteristics to all members of that group. From a semiotic perspective, stereotyping can be seen as a distorted form of synecdoche, in which (in this case) a part stands for a whole. It is also worth noting that many stereotypes are based on visible phenomena and are applied to groups that are distinctive in one way or another and have easily recognizable identities.

Stereotypes can be positive (the kindly, dedicated family doctor), negative (the drunken Irishman) or mixed (the stern but effective teacher). They are not always negative, but they are always oversimplifications and prevent people from seeing individuals as they really are.

Stereotypes are particularly pernicious when they are applied to roles, or the kinds of behaviors that are expected of people relative to the situations in which they find themselves, their places in society, and their status (ranking) in some organization or institution. Scriptwriters make use of stereotypes because they make it relatively easy to define characters and explain motives, but these stereotypes also give readers and viewers of films and television shows distorted images of certain kinds of people. For instance, both the men and women who watch movies and TV programs will, unconsciously, pick up notions from the material they are exposed to about what women should do, how women should act, and how men should be expected to relate to women. Clearly, if all women's roles are limited to drab housewives or mindless sex objects, this can have an effect on male-female relations.

Stereotypes are sometimes used by humorists and are often spread and reinforced by jokes, such as jokes told about various racial and ethnic groups—jokes that are invariably insulting. Ethnic jokes are told all over the world and are used by various groups to attack other groups. Many of the jokes that Americans used to tell about Polish people are still being told in England, but they are told about Irish people. Some groups tell such jokes about themselves, as a means of immunizing themselves against stereotypes and as a way of showing that the jokes have no power to hurt them.

The mass media are often attacked for using stereotypes in the texts they carry and thus causing psychological harm to people in the groups being stereotyped and providing audiences with unrealistic views of representatives of such groups. Can the media function without stereotyping people? Is there something in the nature of the mass media that requires this device, or is stereotyping merely a convenient tool for writers?

Popular Culture

The term *popular culture* resists definition. Some define it as the culture of the ordinary person—the television shows, films, records, radio programs, foods, fashions, magazines, and other phenomena that play important roles in our daily lives. As I have noted previously, there is a good deal of disagreement about what popular culture is and is not and how it relates to "elite" culture.

In the past, popular culture was dismissed by many academics as unworthy of attention. The texts of popular culture were seen as subliterary junk, and those who consumed them were seen as wasting their time. Obviously, from a literary point of view, a comic book cannot compare with a novel by Hemingway or Dostoyevsky. But such comparisons are both unfair and misguided. Scholars who study popular culture are not concerned primarily with aesthetic matters; instead, their interest is in the role that popular culture plays in society—the ideological messages contained in popular culture, the way popular culture socializes young people, the psychological impact of popular culture on individuals, the depiction of women and members of other groups (ethnic, racial, socioeconomic) in popular culture texts, and so on.

Popular culture cannot be equated with the mass media (though much popular culture is transmitted by the media) or with popular genres, though genre literature and dramatic productions are an important component of popular culture. The cinema used to be seen as trivial, but in recent years it has been elevated to the status of an important medium, capable of generating great works of art (although many films are not great art, by any means). A novel can be a work of popular culture or elite culture, depending on who the novelist is. In some cases, works of elite culture influence works of popular culture (for example, many films draw upon myths), whereas in other cases, the influence is reversed (for instance, the cartoon character Krazy Kat was incorporated in a ballet, an elite art form). Some works originally seen as popular culture are later elevated to the status of elite culture (for example, Gershwin's *Porgy and Bess* has in recent years attained the elite status of opera, whereas in the past it was often considered simply "folk opera" or a musical play).

What used to be described as "popular culture criticism" has itself changed, and now the same professors who once described their area of interest as popular culture now describe it as "contemporary culture," or "cultural studies," or "cultural criticism." This is because, it could be argued, the important part of the term is *culture*, not *popular* (a word that eludes easy definition).

The new cultural criticism, informed by a combination of psychoanalytic theory, Marxist theory, semiotic theory, and literary theory, is particularly interested in how texts generate meaning and in the ideological aspects of popular culture, the role it plays in the social and political world, and the role played in society by the people who control the media that carry much of popular culture. Some cultural critics focus great attention on the social and political aspects of popular culture and describe themselves as "critical theorists."

The difference between popular culture critics (many of whom are critical theorists) and scholars who study and analyze the mass media per se is that popular culture critics tend to focus much of their attention on texts—specific works and specific genres—in contrast to mass communication scholars, who are more interested, generally speaking, in the way mass-mediated works affect attitudes, values, beliefs, and related concerns in audiences. Mass communication scholars tend to see themselves as social scientists, and their approach is (or at least was) essentially social psychological, measuring effects, using participant observation, and other such techniques. Popular culture critics draw much of their theory from literary theory, philosophy, rhetorical theory, and related areas.

Popular culture and the mass media play an important part in our everyday lives; indeed, they dominate the everyday lives of some people, those we might characterize as television addicts and mass media junkies. The question of how we define what everyday life is and how it is affected by the media and popular culture is our next topic.

Everyday Life

The study of everyday life involves the focus, by social scientists, on the experiences of ordinary people and on their routines, attitudes, beliefs, and ways of functioning, with a particular interest in how they find meaning in their experiences. Jack D. Douglas and his colleagues, sociologists who have worked in this area, say that "the sociology of everyday life is a sociological orientation concerned with experiencing, observing, understanding, describing, analyzing, and communicating about people interacting in concrete situations" (Douglas et al., 1980, p. 1).

There are, these researchers add, three important points to be made about how sociologists of everyday life work. First, they study social interactions by "observing them in natural situations, that is, in situations that occur independently of scientific manipulation." They work in the everyday world, not in situations that are experimentally controlled. Second, they focus on observing people interacting in face-to-face concrete situations— where people can be found doing things, perceiving things, feeling, and thinking. And third, they focus on the meanings that people find in their lives, in their "internal" experiences, or in what Douglas et al. say are "the feelings, perceptions, emotions, moods, thoughts, ideas, beliefs, values and morals of the members of society" (p. 2). Douglas et al. also make a distinction between "everyday" experiences and "anyday" experiences—the latter referring to things that can happen to a person any day, as contrasted to things that happen to them every day.

Continental social scientists also have an interest in everyday life, though many of them are interested less in the microanalytic

methods of American scholars than in the ideological aspects of
everyday life. Henri Lefebvre (1984) points out that we tend to
neglect the everyday lives of ordinary people. He proposes a
study of what he calls the Quotidian:

> The Quotidian is a philosophical concept that cannot be understood
> outside philosophy; it designates for and by philosophy the non-
> philosophical and is unthinkable in another context; it is a concept
> that neither belongs to nor reflects everyday life, but rather ex-
> presses its possible transfiguration in philosophical terms. (p. 13)

Everyday life is the proper subject of philosophy because, Lefebvre
adds, everyday life is nonphilosophical and directs the philosopher away from traditional subjects toward recurrences and how
the social existence of people is produced.

The task of the student of everyday life, Lefebvre argues, is
to find some kind of meaningful pattern in the everyday lives of
typical people—in their recurring activities, in the objects they
purchase and use, in the news items they read, the advertisements
they hear and see, and so on. Of particular importance is the dis-
covery of the ideological dimensions of our activities and the ideologies carried by the media, with particular attention to the
institution of advertising.

Some American scholars blend the two perspectives, and study
the ways ideological matters structure our everyday interactions
and how we find meaning in life. It is possible to draw a line
between mass-mediated culture and everyday life, though in
some cases this line would be very faint or, according to scholars
such as Lefebvre, nonexistent. He sees everyday life as being
shaped, in great measure, by advertising. Much of everyday life
is obviously permeated by popular culture, if not subsumed
under it. I refer to phenomena such as fads, fashions, styles, and
commonly used expressions, as well as our routine viewing of
television, listening to radio, and reading of newspapers and
magazines.

Whatever the case, everyday life has become the object of
considerable attention by scholars of all persuasions, who study

a wide range of activities: our use of telephones, the way we tip in bars and restaurants, the typical day of the housewife, people who believe in flying saucers, the sociology of the bicycle, the kinds of people who are attracted to religious cults, and more. Our everyday lives can also been seen as stories, as narratives, in which we act out our lives and construct our identities.

Conclusion

It is difficult at times to distinguish among studies of popular culture, studies of mass media, and studies of everyday life. Our everyday lives are, to a great degree, occupied with watching television, listening to radio, reading newspapers and magazines, and attending to other mass media. But we also wear clothes, eat food, and engage in various social rituals that are not mass-mediated per se (though perhaps influenced by mass media). What the sociological perspective does is provide us with a number of tools for analyzing texts and for considering the impacts of these texts (and perhaps of the media themselves, independent of the texts they carry, if McLuhan is correct) on people (audiences) and on society in general. A sociological perspective enhances our understanding of the roles that works of art (of all kinds) play in society and provides cultural critics with a number of concepts that are of considerable importance in carrying out their work.

Suggested Further Reading

Abelove, H., Barale, M. A., & Halperin, D. (Eds.). (1993). *The lesbian and gay studies reader*. New York: Routledge.

Adorno, T. W. (1967). *Prisms* (S. Weber & S. Weber, Trans.). Cambridge: MIT Press.

Adorno, T. W. (1991). *The culture industry: Selected essays on mass culture*. London: Routledge.

Armstrong, N. (1987). *Desire and domestic fiction: A political history of the novel*. New York: Oxford University Press.

Aronowitz, S. (1992). *The politics of identity*. New York: Routledge.

Aronowitz, S. (1993). *Dead artists, live theories and other cultural problems*. New York: Routledge.

Bakhtin, M. (1984). *Rabelais and his world* (H. Iswolsky, Trans.). Bloomington: Indiana University Press.

Barker, M., & Beezer, A. (1992). *Reading into cultural studies*. London: Routledge.

Barthes, R. (1970). *Writing degree zero and elements of semiology* (A. Lavers & C. Smith, Trans.). Boston: Beacon.

Barthes, R. (1974). *S/Z* (R. Miller, Trans.). New York: Hill & Wang.

Barthes, R. (1975). *The pleasure of the text* (R. Miller, Trans.). New York: Hill & Wang.

Barthes, R. (1975). *Roland Barthes by Roland Barthes* (R. Howard, Trans.). New York: Hill & Wang.

Barthes, R. (1978). *A lover's discourse* (R. Howard, Trans.). New York: Hill & Wang.

Barthes, R. (1988). *The semiotic challenge* (R. Howard, Trans.). New York: Hill & Wang.

Bateson, G. (1972). *Steps to an ecology of mind*. New York: Ballantine.

Baudrillard, J. (1983). *Simulations* (P. Foss et al., Trans.). New York: Semiotext(e).

Beilharz, P., Robinson, G., & Rundell, J. (1992). *Between totalitarianism and postmodernity: A thesis eleven reader*. Cambridge: MIT Press.

Benjamin, W. (1974). The work of art in the age of mechanical reproduction. In Mast, G., & Cohen, M. (Eds.), *Film theory and criticism*. New York: Oxford University Press.

Bennett, T., & Woollacott, J. (1987). *Bond and beyond: The political career of a popular hero*. New York: Methuen.

Berger, A. A. (1973). *The comic-stripped American*. New York: Walker.

Berger, A. A. (1984). *Signs in contemporary culture: An introduction to semiotics*. New York: Annenberg-Longman.

Berger, A. A. (Ed.). (1987). *Visual sociology and semiotics*. Aachen, Germany: Edition Herodot.

Berger, A. A. (1989). *Seeing is believing: An introduction to visual communication*. Mountain View, CA: Mayfield.

Berger, A. A. (Ed.). (1990). *Agitpop: Political culture and communication theory*. New Brunswick, NJ: Transaction.

Berger, A. A. (1993). *An anatomy of humor*. New Brunswick, NJ: Transaction.

Berman, M. (1982). *All that is solid melts into air: The experience of modernity*. New York: Touchstone.

Bernstein, R. J. (1992). *The new constellation: The ethical-political horizons of modernity/postmodernity*. Cambridge: MIT Press.

Bettelheim, B. (1976). *The uses of enchantment: The meaning and importance of fairy tales*. New York: Knopf.

Bhabha, H. K. (1993). *The location of culture*. New York: Routledge.

Bird, J., et al. (1993). *Mapping the futures: Local cultures, global change*. London: Routledge.

Blau, H. (1992). *To all appearances: Ideology and performance*. London: Routledge.

Bloom, C. (Ed.). (1993). *Creepers: British horror and fantasy in the twentieth century*. Boulder, CO: Westview.

Bourdieu, P., & Passeron, J.-C. (1990). *Reproduction in education, society, and culture*. Newbury Park, CA: Sage.

Bowlby, R. (1993). *Shopping with Freud: Items on consumerism, feminism and psychoanalysis*. London: Routledge.

Branigan, E. (1992). *Narrative comprehension and film*. New York: Routledge.

Brenkman, J. (1993). *Straight, male, modern: A cultural critique of psychoanalysis*. New York: Routledge.

Brown, M. E. (Ed.). (1990). *Television and women's culture: The politics of the popular*. Newbury Park, CA: Sage.

Buck-Morss, S. (1989). *The dialectics of seeing: Walter Benjamin and the arcades project*. Minneapolis: University of Minnesota Press.

Butler, J. (1993). *Bodies that matter*. New York: Routledge.

Carey, J. W. (Ed.). (1988). *Media, myths, and narratives: Television and the press*. Newbury Park, CA: Sage.

Clark, K., & Holmquist, M. (1984). *Mikhail Bakhtin*. Cambridge, MA: Harvard University Press.

Clarke, J. (1992). *New times and old enemies: Essays on cultural studies and America.* London: Routledge.

Collins, J., Radner, H., & Collins, A. P. (Eds.). (1992). *Film theory goes to the movies: Cultural analysis of contemporary film.* New York: Routledge.

Collins, R., Curran, J., Garnham, N., Scannell, P., Schlesinger, P., & Sparks, C. (Eds.). (1986). *Media, culture and society: A critical reader.* London: Sage.

Cottom, D. (1989). *Text and culture: The politics of interpretation.* Minneapolis: University of Minnesota Press.

Coward, R., & Ellis, J. (1977). *Language and materialism: Developments in semiology and the theory of the subject.* London: Routledge & Kegan Paul.

Crane, D. (1992). *The production of culture: Media and the urban arts.* Newbury Park, CA: Sage.

Creed, B. (1993). *The monstrous-feminine: Film, feminism, psychoanalysis.* London: Routledge.

Crimp, D. (Ed.). (1988). *AIDS: Cultural analysis/cultural activism.* Cambridge: MIT Press.

Crook, S., Pakulski, J., & Waters, M. (Eds.). (1992). *Postmodernization: Change in advanced society.* London: Sage.

Cross, G. (1993). *Time and money: The making of a consumer culture.* London: Routledge.

Culler, J. (1977). *Ferdinand de Saussure.* New York: Penguin.

Culler, J. (1981). *The pursuit of signs.* Ithaca, NY: Cornell University Press.

Culler, J. (1982). *On deconstruction.* Ithaca, NY: Cornell University Press.

Davis, R. C., & Schleifer, R. (1991). *Criticism and culture.* London: Longman.

de Certeau, M. (1984). *The practice of everyday life* (S. Rendall, Trans.). Berkeley: University of California Press.

de Certeau, M. (1986). *Heterologies: Discourse on the other* (B. Massumi, Trans.). Minneapolis: University of Minnesota Press.

De Lauretis, T. (1984). *Alice doesn't: Feminism, semiotics, cinema.* Bloomington: Indiana University Press.

De Lauretis, T. (1987). *Technologies of gender: Essays on theory, film and fiction.* Bloomington: Indiana University Press.

Denzin, N. K. (1991). *Images of postmodern society: Social theory and contemporary cinema.* London: Sage.

Derrida, J. (1967). *Of grammatology* (G. C. Spivak, Trans.). Baltimore: Johns Hopkins University Press.

Derrida, J. (1981). *Positions* (A. Bass, Trans.). Chicago: University of Chicago Press.

Doane, M. A. (1987). *The desire to desire: The woman's film of the 1940s.* Bloomington: Indiana University Press.

Doane, M. A. (1991). *Femmes fatales.* New York: Routledge.

Douglas, M. (1992). *Risk and blame: Essays in cultural theory.* London: Routledge.

Dundes, A. (1987). *Cracking jokes: Studies in sick humor cycles and stereotypes.* Berkeley, CA: Ten Speed.

Dworkin, D. L., & Roman, L. G. (1992). *Views beyond the border country: Raymond Williams and cultural politics.* New York: Routledge.

Dyer, R. (1993). *The matter of images: Essays on representations.* London: Routledge.

Eagleton, T. (1976). *Marxism and literary criticism.* Berkeley: University of California Press.

Eagleton, T. (1983). *Literary theory: An introduction.* Minneapolis: University of Minnesota Press.

Easthope, A. (1991). *Literary into cultural studies.* London: Routledge.

Ehrmann, J. (Ed.). (1970). *Structuralism.* Garden City, NY: Anchor.

Elam, K. (1980). *The semiotics of theatre and drama.* London: Methuen.

Ewen, S. (1976). *Captains of consciousness.* New York: McGraw-Hill.

Ewen, S., & Ewen, E. (1992). *Channels of desire: Mass images and the shaping of American consciousness* (rev. ed.). Minneapolis: University of Minnesota Press.

Featherstone, M. (1991). *Consumer culture and postmodernism.* London: Sage.

Ferguson, R., Gever, M., Minh-ha, T. T., & West, C. (Eds.). (1990). *Out there: Marginalization and contemporary cultures.* Cambridge: MIT Press.

Fiske, J. (1989). *Reading the popular.* Winchester, MA: Unwin Hyman.

Fiske, J. (1989). *Understanding popular culture.* Winchester, MA: Unwin Hyman.

Fjellman, S. M. (1992). *Vinyl leaves: Walt Disney World and America.* Boulder, CO: Westview.

Franklin, S., Lury, C., & Stacey, J. (1992). *Off-centre: Feminism and cultural studies.* London: Routledge.

Freud, S. (1957). *Civilization and its discontents* (J. Riviere, Trans.). London: Hogarth.

Freud, S. (1963). *Jokes and their relation to the unconscious* (J. Strachey, Trans.). New York: W. W. Norton.

Fry, W. F. (1968). *Sweet madness: A study of humor.* Palo Alto, CA: Pacific.

Frye, N. (1957). *Anatomy of criticism.* Princeton, NJ: Princeton University Press.

Garber, M. (1993). *Vested interests: Cross-dressing and cultural anxiety.* New York: Harper Perennial.

Garber, M., Matlock, J., & Walkowitz, R. (Eds.). (1993). *Media spectacles.* New York: Routledge.

Garber, M., Parmar, P., & Greyson, J. (Eds.). (1993). *Queer looks: Perspectives on lesbian and gay film and video.* New York: Routledge.

Glasgow Media Group. (1976). *Bad news.* London: Routledge & Kegan Paul.

Glasgow Media Group. (1980). *More bad news.* London: Routledge & Kegan Paul.

Goldstein, A., Jacob, M. J., Rorimer, A., & Singerman, H. (1989). *A forest of signs: Art in the crisis of representation.* Cambridge: MIT Press.

Greenblatt, S. J. (1992). *Learning to curse: Essays in early modern culture.* New York: Routledge.

Gronbeck, B., Farrell, T. J., & Soukup, P. A. (Eds.). (1991). *Media, consciousness, and culture: Explorations of Walter Ong's thought.* Newbury Park, CA: Sage.

Grossberg, L. (1992). *We gotta get out of this place: Popular conservatism and post-modern culture.* New York: Routledge.

Grossberg, L., Nelson, C., & Treichler, P. A. (Eds.). (1992). *Cultural studies.* New York: Routledge.

Guiraud, P. (1975). *Semiology.* London: Routledge & Kegan Paul.

Gumbrecht, H. U. (1992). *Making sense in life and literature* (G. Burns, Trans.). Minneapolis: University of Minnesota Press.

Habermas, J. (1979). *Communication and the evolution of society* (T. McCarthy, Trans.). Boston: Beacon.

Habermas, J. (1987). *The philosophical discourse on modernity: Twelve lectures* (F. G. Lawrence, Trans.). Minneapolis: University of Minnesota Press.

Habermas, J. (1989). *The new conservatism: Cultural criticism and the historians' debate* (S. W. Nicholsen, Trans.). Minneapolis: University of Minnesota Press.

Haug, W. F. (1971). *Critique of commodity aesthetics: Appearance, sexuality, and advertising in capitalist society* (R. Bock, Trans.). Minneapolis: University of Minnesota Press.

Hoggart, R. (1992). *The uses of literacy.* New Brunswick, NJ: Transaction.

Holland, N. (1975). *Five readers reading.* New Haven, CT: Yale University Press.

Hoover, S. M. (1988). *Mass media religion: The social sources of the electronic church.* Newbury Park, CA: Sage.

Hutcheon, L. (1989). *The politics of postmodernism.* London: Routledge.

Jakobson, R. (1985). *Verbal art, verbal sign, verbal time* (K. Pomorska & S. Rudy, Eds.). Minneapolis: University of Minnesota Press.

Jameson, F. (1971). *Marxism and form: Twentieth century dialectical theories of literature.* Princeton, NJ: Princeton University Press.

Jameson, F. (1981). *The political unconscious.* Ithaca, NY: Cornell University Press.

Jameson, F. (1992). *The geopolitical aesthetic: Cinema and space in the world system.* Bloomington: Indiana University Press.

Jameson, F. (1992). *Signatures of the visible.* New York: Routledge.

Jauss, H. R. (1982). *Aesthetic experience and literary hermeneutics* (M. Shaw, Trans.). Minneapolis: University of Minnesota Press.

Jauss, H. R. (1982). *Toward an aesthetic of reception* (T. Bahti, Trans.). Minneapolis: University of Minnesota Press.

Jensen, J. (1990). *Redeeming modernity: Contradictions in media criticism.* Newbury Park, CA: Sage.

Jhally, S., & Lewis, J. (1992). *Enlightened racism: The Cosby Show, audiences, and the myth of the American dream.* Boulder, CO: Westview.

Jones, S. (1992). *Rock formation: Music, technology, and mass communication.* Newbury Park, CA: Sage.

Jowett, G., & Linton, J. M. (1989). *Movies as mass communication.* Newbury Park: Sage.

Kaplan, E. A. (1982). *Motherhood and representation.* London: Routledge.

Kellner, D. (1992). *The Persian Gulf TV war.* Boulder, CO: Westview.

Korzenny, F., & Ting-Toomey, S. (Eds.). (1992). *Mass media effects across cultures.* Newbury Park, CA: Sage.

Larsen, N. (1989). *Modernism and hegemony: A materialist critique of aesthetic agencies.* Minneapolis: University of Minnesota Press.

Lavers, A. (1982). *Roland Barthes: Structuralism and after.* Cambridge, MA: Harvard University Press.

Lipsitz, G. (1990). *Time passages: Collective memory and American popular culture.* Minneapolis: University of Minnesota Press.

Lotman, J. M. (1976). *Semiotics of cinema.* Ann Arbor: Michigan Slavic Contributions.

Lotman, J. M. (1991). *Universe of the mind: A semiotic theory of culture.* Bloomington: Indiana University Press.

Lyotard, J.-F. (1984). *The postmodern condition: A report on knowledge.* Minneapolis: University of Minnesota Press.

MacCabe, C. (1985). *Tracking the signifier: Theoretical essays on film, linguistics, and literature.* Minneapolis: University of Minnesota Press.

MacCannell, D., & MacCannell, J. F. (1982). *The time of the sign: A semiotic interpretation of modern culture.* Bloomington: Indiana University Press.

Mandel, E. (1985). *Delightful murder: A social history of the crime story.* Minneapolis: University of Minnesota Press.

Massumi, B. (1992). *A user's guide to capitalism and schizophrenia: Deviations from Deleuze and Guattari.* Cambridge: MIT Press.

Mattelart, A., & Mattelart, M. (1992). *Rethinking media theory* (J. A. Cohen & M. Urquidi, Trans.). Minneapolis: University of Minnesota Press.

McCarthy, T. (1991). *Ideals and illusions: On reconstruction and deconstruction in contemporary critical theory.* Cambridge: MIT Press.

McClue, G. (1993). *Dark knights: The new comics in context.* Boulder, CO: Westview.

Mellencamp, P. (1990). *Indiscretions: Avant-garde film, video and feminism.* Bloomington: Indiana University Press.

Mellencamp, P. (Ed.). (1990). *Logics of television: Essays in cultural criticism.* Bloomington: Indiana University Press.

Metz, C. (1982). *The imaginary signifier: Psychoanalysis and the cinema* (C. Britton et al., Trans.). Bloomington: Indiana University Press.

Mindess, H. (1971). *Laughter and liberation.* Los Angeles: Nash.

Modleski, T. (1984). *Loving with a vengeance: Mass-produced fantasies for women.* New York: Routledge.

Modleski, T. (Ed.). (1986). *Studies in entertainment: Critical approaches to mass culture.* Bloomington: Indiana University Press.

Modleski, T. (1988). *The women who knew too much: Hitchcock and feminist theory.* New York: Routledge.

Mulvey, L. (1989). *Visual and other pleasures.* Bloomington: Indiana University Press.

Naremore, J., & Brantlinger, P. (Eds.). (1991). *Modernity and mass culture.* Bloomington: Indiana University Press.

Navarro, D. (Ed.). (1993, Summer). Postmodernism: Center and periphery [Special issue]. *South Atlantic Quarterly*.

Nichols, B. (1981). *Ideology and the image: Social representation in the cinema and other media*. Bloomington: Indiana University Press.

Nichols, B. (1992). *Representing reality: Issues and concepts in documentary*. Bloomington: Indiana University Press.

Penley, C. (1989). *The future of an illusion: Film, feminism, and psychoanalysis*. Minneapolis: University of Minnesota Press.

Piddington, R. (1963). *The psychology of laughter*. New York: Gamut.

Powell, C., & Paton, G. E. C. (Eds.). (1988). *Humor in society: Resistance and control*. New York: St. Martin's.

Prindle, D. F. (1993). *Risky business: The political economy of Hollywood*. Boulder, CO: Westview.

Propp, V. (1984). *Theory and history of folklore* (A. Y. Martin & R. P. Martin, Trans.). Minneapolis: University of Minnesota Press.

Ramet, S. P. (Ed.). (1993). *Rocking the state: Rock music and politics in Eastern Europe and the Soviet Union*. Boulder, CO: Westview.

Real, M. R. (1989). *Supermedia: A cultural studies approach*. Newbury Park, CA: Sage.

Reinelt, J. G., & Roach, J. R. (Eds.). (1993). *Critical theory and performance*. Ann Arbor: University of Michigan Press.

Richter, M., & Bakken, H. (1992). *The cartoonist's muse: A guide to generating and developing creative ideas*. Chicago: Contemporary Books.

Rouch, I., & Carr, G. F. (Eds.). (1989). *The semiotic bridge: Trends from California*. Berlin: Mouton de Gruyter.

Ryan, M., & Kellner, D. M. (1988). *Camera politica: The politics and ideology of contemporary Hollywood film*. Bloomington: Indiana University Press.

Sabin, R. (1993). *Adult comics: An introduction*. London: Routledge.

Said, E. (1983). *The world, the text, and the critic*. Cambridge, MA: Harvard University Press.

Saint-Martin, F. (1990). *Semiotics of visual language*. Bloomington: Indiana University Press.

Schechner, R. (1993). *The future of ritual: Writings on culture and performance*. London: Routledge.

Schneider, C., & Wallis, B. (Eds.). (1989). *Global television*. Cambridge: MIT Press.

Schostak, J. (1993). *Dirty marks: The education of self, media and popular culture*. Boulder, CO: Westview.

Schwichtenberg, C. (Ed.). (1992). *The Madonna connection: Representational politics, subcultural identities, and cultural theory*. Boulder, CO: Westview.

Sebeok, T. (Ed.). (1978). *Sight, sound and sense*. Bloomington: Indiana University Press.

Shukman, A. (1977). *Literature and semiotics: A study of the writings of Yuri M. Lotman*. Amsterdam: North-Holland.

Smith, G. (Ed.). (1991). *On Walter Benjamin: Critical essays and recollections*. Cambridge: MIT Press.

Smith, P. (1988). *Discerning the subject*. Minneapolis: University of Minnesota Press.

Spivak, G. C. (1992). *Outside in the teaching machine*. New York: Routledge.

Staake, B. (1991). *The complete book of caricature*. Cincinnati, OH: North Light.

Steidman, S. (1993). *Romantic longings: Love in America 1830-1980*. New York: Routledge.

Szondi, P. (1986). *On textual understanding* (H. Mendelsohn, Trans.). Minneapolis: University of Minnesota Press.

Todorov, T. (1975). *The fantastic: A structural approach to a literary genre* (R. Howard, Trans.). Ithaca, NY: Cornell University Press.

Todorov, T. (1981). *Introduction to poetics* (R. Howard, Trans.). Minneapolis: University of Minnesota Press.

Todorov, T. (1984). *Mikhail Bakhtin: The dialogical principle*. Minneapolis: University of Minnesota Press.

Traube, E. G. (1992). *Dreaming identities: Class, gender, and generation in 1980s Hollywood movies*. Boulder, CO: Westview.

Turner, B. S. (1990). *Theories of modernity and postmodernity*. London: Sage.

Wernick, A. (1991). *Promotional culture*. London: Sage.

Willemen, P. (1993). *Looks and frictions: Essays in cultural studies and film theory*. Bloomington: Indiana University Press.

Williams, R. (1958). *Culture and society: 1780-1950*. New York: Columbia University Press.

Williams, R. (1976). *Keywords*. New York: Oxford University Press.

Williamson, J. (1978). *Decoding advertisements: Ideology and meaning in advertising*. London: Marion Boyars.

Willis, P. (1990). *Common culture: Symbolic work at play in the everyday cultures of the young*. Boulder, CO: Westview.

Winick, C. (1968). *The new people: Desexualization in American life*. New York: Pegasus.

Wollen, P. (1993). *Raiding the icebox: Reflections on twentieth-century culture*. Bloomington: Indiana University Press.

Wright, W. (1975). *Sixguns and society: A structural study of the western*. Berkeley: University of California Press.

Zizek, S. (1991). *Looking awry: An introduction to Jacques Lacan through popular culture*. Cambridge: MIT Press.

References

Abrams, M. H. (1958). *The mirror and the lamp: Romantic theory and the critical tradition*. New York: W. W. Norton.

Abrams, M. H. (1989). The deconstructive angel. In R. C. Davis & R. Schleifer (Eds.), *Contemporary literary criticism: Literary and cultural studies* (2nd ed.). New York: Longman.

Adorno, T. W. (1948). *Philosophy of modern music*. New York: Seabury.

Adorno, T. W. (1957). Television and the patterns of mass culture. In B. Rosenberg & D. M. White (Eds.), *Mass culture: The popular arts in America*. New York: Free Press.

Bakhtin, M. M. (1981). *The dialogic imagination* (M. Holmquist, Ed.; C. Emerson & M. Holmquist, Trans.). Austin: University of Texas Press.

Barthes, R. (1972). *Mythologies* (A. Lavers, Trans.). New York: Hill & Wang.

Barthes, R. (1982). *Empire of signs* (R. Howard, Trans.) New York: Hill & Wang.

Benjamin, W. (1974). The work of art in the age of mechanical reproduction. In G. Mast & M. Cohen (Eds.), *Film theory and criticism: Introductory readings*. Oxford: Oxford University Press.

Berger, A. A. (1991). *Media analysis techniques* (rev. ed.). Newbury Park, CA: Sage.

Best, S., & Kellner, D. M. (1991). *Postmodern theory: Critical interrogations*. New York: Guilford.

Brenner, C. (1974). *An elementary textbook of psychoanalysis* (rev. ed.). Garden City, NY: Anchor.

Cirksena, K. (1987). Politics and difference: Radical feminist epistemological premises for communication studies. *Journal of Communication Inquiry, 11*, 19-28.

Culler, J. (1975). *Structuralist poetics: Structuralism, linguistics, and the study of literature*. Ithaca, NY: Cornell University Press.

Dorfman, A., & Mattelart, A. (1991). *How to read Donald Duck: Imperialist ideology in the Disney comic* (2nd ed.) (D. Kunzle, Trans.). New York: International General.

Douglas, J. D., Adler, P. A., Adler, P., Fontana, A., Freeman, C. R., & Kotarba, J. A. (1980). *Introduction to the sociologies of everyday life.* Boston: Allyn & Bacon.

Douglas, M. (1975). *Implicit meanings: Essays in anthropology.* London: Routledge & Kegan Paul.

Durkheim, É. (1951). *Suicide.* New York: Free Press.

Durkheim, É. (1967). *The elementary forms of the religious life.* New York: Free Press.

Eco, U. (1976). *A theory of semiotics.* Bloomington: Indiana University Press.

Eco, U. (1984). *The role of the reader.* Bloomington: Indiana University Press.

Eisenstein, S. (1947). Word and image. In S. Eisenstein, *The film sense* (J. Leyda, Ed. & Trans.). New York: Harcourt, Brace.

Eliade, M. (1961). *The sacred and the profane: The nature of religion* (W. Trask, Trans.). New York: Harper & Row.

Engels, F. (1972). Socialism: Utopian and scientific. In R. Tucker (Ed.), *The Marx-Engels reader.* New York: W. W. Norton.

Enzenberger, H. M. (1974). *The consciousness industry: On literature, politics and the media.* New York: Seabury.

Fairchild, H. P. (Ed.). (1967). *Dictionary of sociology and related terms.* Totowa, NJ: Littlefield, Adams.

Featherstone, M. (1988). In pursuit of the postmodern: An introduction. In M. Featherstone (Ed.), Postmodernism [Special issue]. *Theory, Culture & Society, 5,* 195-213.

Fiske, J., & Hartley, J. (1978). *Reading television.* London: Methuen.

Freud, S. (1933). *New introductory lectures on psychoanalysis* (J. Strachey, Trans.). New York: W. W. Norton.

Freud, S. (1953). *A general introduction to psychoanalysis.* Garden City, NY: Doubleday.

Freud, S. (1962). *Civilization and its discontents.* New York: W. W. Norton.

Freud, S. (1963). The occurrence in dreams of material from fairy-tales. In S. Freud, *Character and culture: Psychoanalysis applied to anthropology, mythology, folklore, literature, and culture in general* (P. Rieff, Ed.). New York: Collier.

Freud, S. (1965). *The interpretation of dreams* (J. Strachey, Trans.). New York: Avon.

Fromm, E. (1957). *The forgotten language: An introduction to the understanding of dreams, fairy tales and myths.* New York: Grove.

Fromm, E. (1980). *The greatness and limitations of Freud's thought.* New York: Mentor.

Gaines, J. (1987). Women and representation: Can we enjoy alternative pleasure? In D. Lazere (Ed.), *American media and mass culture: New left perspectives.* Berkeley: University of California Press.

Gandelman, C. (1991). *Reading pictures, viewing texts.* Bloomington: Indiana University Press.

Gerbner, G. (1977). Comparative cultural indicators. In G. Gerbner (Ed.), *Mass media politics in changing cultures.* New York: John Wiley.

Girard, R. (1991). *A theatre of envy: William Shakespeare*. Oxford: Oxford University Press.

Gitlin, T. (1989, July/August). Postmodernism defined, at last! *Utne Reader*, pp. 52-58, 61.

Gramsci, A. (1957). *The modern prince and other writings* (L. Marks, Ed. & Trans.). New York: International.

Grotjahn, M. (1966). *Beyond laughter: Humor and the subconscious*. New York: McGraw-Hill.

Haug, W. F. (1987). *Commodity aesthetics: Ideology and culture*. New York: International General.

Hawkes, T. (1977). *Structuralism and semiotics*. Berkeley: University of California Press.

Henderson, J. L. (1968). Ancient myths and modern man. In C. G. Jung (Ed.), *Man and his symbols*. New York: Dell.

Hinsie, L., & Campbell, R. J. (1970). *Psychiatric dictionary* (4th ed.). New York: Oxford University Press.

Ingarden, R. (1968). *Vom Erkennen des literarischen Kuntswerks*. Tubingen, Germany: n.p.

Iser, W. (1988). The reading process: A phenomenological approach. In D. Lodge (Ed.), *Modern criticism and theory: A reader*. White Plains, NY: Longman. (Original work published 1972)

Jakobson, R. (1988). The metaphoric and metonymic poles. In D. Lodge (Ed.), *Modern criticism and theory: A reader*. White Plains, NY: Longman.

Jameson, F. (1972). *The prison-house of language: A critical account of structuralism and Russian formalism*. Princeton, NJ: Princeton University Press.

Jones, E. (1949). *Hamlet and Oedipus*. New York: W. W. Norton.

Jung, C. G. (1968). Approaching the unconscious. In C. G. Jung (Ed.), *Man and his symbols*. New York: Dell.

Kottak, C. P. (1987). *Cultural anthropology* (4th ed.). New York: Random House.

Lacan, J. (1966). *Ecrits: A selection* (A. Sheridan, Trans.). New York: W. W. Norton.

Lakoff, G., & Johnson, M. (1980). *Metaphors we live by*. Chicago: University of Chicago Press.

Lazere, D. (1977). Mass culture, political consciousness and English studies. *College English, 38*, 755-766.

Le Bon, G. (1960). *The crowd: A study of the popular mind*. New York: Viking. (Original work published 1895)

Lefebvre, H. (1984). *Everyday life in the modern world* (S. Rabinovitch, Trans.). New Brunswick, NJ: Transaction.

Lévi-Strauss, C. (1967). *Structural anthropology*. Garden City, NY: Doubleday.

Lotman, J. M. (1977). *The structure of the artistic text*. Ann Arbor: Michigan Slavic Contributions.

Lowery, S., & DeFleur, M. L. (1983). *Milestones in mass communication research: Media effects*. White Plains, NY: Longman.

Mannheim, K. (1936). *Ideology and utopia: An introduction to the sociology of knowledge* (L. Wirth & E. Shils, Trans.). New York: Harcourt, Brace.

Marx, K. (1963). *Karl Marx: Early writings* (T. B. Bottomore, Ed. & Trans.). New York: McGraw-Hill.

Marx, K. (1964). *Selected writings in sociology and social philosophy* (T. B. Bottomore & M. Rubel, Eds.; T. B. Bottomore, Trans.). New York: McGraw-Hill.

Marx, K. (1972). *Capital*. In R. C. Tucker (Ed.), *The Marx-Engels reader*. New York: W. W. Norton.

McLuhan, M. (1951). *The mechanical bride: Folklore of industrial man*. Boston: Beacon.

McLuhan, M. (1965). *Understanding media: The extensions of man*. New York: McGraw-Hill.

Merton, R. (1957). *Social theory and social structure*. New York: Free Press.

Mueller, C. (1973). *The politics of communication: A study in the political sociology of language, socialization and legitimation*. New York: Oxford University Press.

Nason, S. (1992, April 21). Top 1% had greater net worth than bottom 90% of U.S. households by 1989. *New York Times*.

Noelle-Neumann, E. (1974). The spiral of silence: A theory of public opinion. *Journal of Communication, 24*(2), 43-51.

Peirce, C. S. (1931-1935). *The collected papers of C. S. Pierce* (Vols. 1-6) (C. Hartshorne & P. Weiss, Eds.). Cambridge, MA: Harvard University Press.

Peirce, C. S. (1958). *The collected papers of C. S. Pierce* (Vols. 7-8) (A. W. Burks, Ed.). Cambridge, MA: Harvard University Press.

Propp, V. (1968). *The morphology of the folktale* (2nd ed.). Austin: University of Texas Press. (Original work published 1928)

Pye, L. (1962). *Politics, personality and nation building: Burma's search for identity*. New Haven, CT: Yale University Press.

Saussure, F. de. (1966). *A course in general linguistics* (W. Baskin, Trans.). New York: McGraw-Hill.

Scholes, R. (1974). *Structuralism in literature*. New Haven, CT: Yale University Press.

Schwartz, T. (1974). *The responsive chord*. Garden City, NY: Doubleday.

Sebeok, T. A. (Ed.). (1977). *A perfusion of signs*. Bloomington: Indiana University Press.

Shklovsky, V. (1989). Art as technique. In R. C. Davis & R. Schleifer (Eds.), *Contemporary literary criticism: Literary and cultural studies* (2nd ed.). New York: Longman.

Shorer, M. (1968). The necessity of myth. In H. A. Murray (Ed.), *Myth and mythmaking*. Boston: Beacon.

Silverman, K. (1983). *The subject of semiotics*. New York: Oxford University Press.

Smith, J. H., & Parks, E. W. (1951). *The great critics: An anthology of literary criticism* (3rd ed.). New York: W. W. Norton.

Thompson, M., Ellis, R., & Wildavsky, A. B. (1990). *Cultural theory*. Boulder, CO: Westview.

Tocqueville, A. de. (1956). *Democracy in America* (R. D. Heffner, Ed.). New York: Mentor.

Tönnies, F. (1957). *Community and society (Gemeinschaft und Gesellschaft)* (C. P. Loomis, Ed. & Trans.). East Lansing: Michigan State University Press. (Original work published 1887)

von Franz, M.-L. (1968). The process of individuation. In C. G. Jung (Ed.), *Man and his symbols.* New York: Dell.

Warner, W. L. (1953). *American life: Dream and reality.* Chicago: University of Chicago Press.

Wildavsky, A. B. (1989). Choosing preferences by constructing institutions: A cultural theory of preference formation. In A. A. Berger (Ed.), *Political culture and public opinion.* New Brunswick, NJ: Transaction.

Williams, R. (1977). *Marxism and literature.* New York: Oxford University Press.

Wollen, P. (1973). *Signs and meaning in the cinema.* Bloomington: Indiana University Press.

Zeyman, J. J. (1977). Peirce's theory of signs. In T. A. Sebeok (Ed.), *A perfusion of signs.* Bloomington: Indiana University Press.

Name Index

Abrams, M. H., 12, 13, 14, 25
Adorno, Theodor W., 6, 43, 44
Agamemnon, 110
Allen, Mitch, xi
Allen, Woody, 58
Althusser, Louis, 6, 29, 58
Aristotle, 10, 11, 33, 55, 140
Auden, W. H., 7, 103

Bakhtin, Mikhail, 2, 6, 35, 36, 91, 92, 142
Barthelme, Donald, 28
Barthes, Roland, 6, 29, 72, 84, 85, 142
Bartok, Bela, 27
Baudrillard, Jean, 28
Bazin, Andre, 6
Benjamin, Walter, 6, 65, 66
Bergman, Ingmar, 92
Berkeley, Busby, 31
Berkeley, George, 23, 81
Bluebeard, 131
Bond, James, 63, 84
Bourdieu, Pierre, 6
Braque, Georges, 27
Brecht, Bertolt, 6, 33

Brenner, Charles, 105, 107, 108, 110
Brooks, Cleanth, 19
Burroughs, William, 28
Byrne, David, 28

Campbell, R. J., 104, 106, 112
Cervantes, Miguel de, 142
Chandler, Raymond, 17
Chaplin, Charlie, 18
Christ, Jesus, 80
Cinderella, 24
Cirksena, Kathryn, 30
Comte, Auguste, 134
Crane, Diana, 3
Craze, Sophy, xi
Culler, Jonathan, 97, 98

DeFleur, Melvin L., 153
DeLillo, Don, 28
Derrida, Jacques, 2, 4, 6, 24, 25, 28, 142
Descartes, René, 81
Dietrich, Marlene, 31
Disney, Walt, 62

179

Subject Index

About the Author

Arthur Asa Berger is Professor of Broadcast & Electronic Communication Arts at San Francisco State University, where he has taught since 1965. He has written extensively on popular culture, the mass media, and related concerns. Among his many books are *Media Analysis Techniques* (revised edition, 1991), *Agitpop: Political Culture and Communication Theory* (1990), *Seeing Is Believing* (1989), *Popular Culture Genres* (1992), and *An Anatomy of Humor* (Transaction, 1993). He is a film and television review editor for *Society* magazine, editor of a series of reprints, "Classics in Communications," for Transaction Books, and a consulting editor for *Humor* magazine. He has appeared on *20/20* and *The Today Show*, and appears frequently on various local television and radio programs in the San Francisco area. *Cultural Criticism* is his twenty-fourth book and sixth book for Sage Publications.